Who Calls the Shots on the New York Stages?

Contemporary Theatre Studies

A series of books edited by Franc Chamberlain, Nene College, UK

This book is part of a series. The publisher will accept continuation orders which may be cancelled at any time and which provide for automatic billing and shipping of each title in the series upon publication. Please write for details.

Who Calls the Shots on the New York Stages?

Kalina Stefanova-Peteva

h⚫ap **harwood academic publishers**
Switzerland • Australia • Belgium • France • Germany • Gt. Britain
India • Japan • Malaysia • Netherlands • Russia • Singapore • USA

Harwood Academic Publishers

Private Bag 8
Camberwell, Victoria 3124
Australia

12, Cour Saint-Eloi
75012 Paris
France

Christburger Str. 11
10405 Berlin
Germany

Post Office Box 90
Reading, Berkshire RG1 8JL
United Kingdom

3-14-9, Okubo
Shinjuku, Tokyo 169
Japan

Emmaplein 5
1075 AW Amsterdam
Netherlands

820 Town Center Drive
Langhorne, PA 19047
United States of America

Library of Congress Cataloging-in-Publication Data

Stefanova-Peteva, Kalina, 1962–
        Who calls the shots on the New York stages? / Kalina Stefanova
    –Peteva
            p. cm. -- (Contemporary theatre studies, ISSN 1049-6513; V.
    4)
        Includes index.
        ISBN 3-7186-5437-7 (hb) : $42.00. -- ISBN 3-7186-5438-5 (sb) :
    $18.00
        1. Dramatic criticism -- New York (N.Y.) 2. Theater -- New York
    (N.Y.) -- History -- 20th century. 3. Theater critics -- New York (N.Y.) --
    Interviews.   I. Title   II. Series.
    PN1707.S74 1992
    792' 09747' 109045 -- dc20   93-34934
                                                                        CIP

CONTENTS

PART V: INTERMISSION WITH A FROWN

PART VI: THUMBS UP!

To my Mother

LIST OF INTERVIEWEES

NEW YORK DRAMA CRITICS:

Stanley Kauffmann
Walter Kerr   - the veterans
Glenn Loney
Gordon Rogoff

Clive Barnes   - *New York Post*
Robert Brustein   - *The New Republic*
Dennis Cunningham   - *WCBS - TV*
Michael Feingold   - *The Village Voice*
Jeremy Gerard   - *Variety*
Mel Gussow   - *The New York Times*
William A. Henry III   - *Time*
Holly Hill   - a correspondent of
                                      The Times of London for
                                      the New York theater
Jonathan Kalb   - *The Village Voice*
Howard Kissel   - *New York Daily News*
Stewart Klein   - *Fox - 5*
Jack Kroll   - *Newsweek*
Pia Lindstrom   - *WNBC - TV*
Edith Oliver   - *The New Yorker*
Frank Rich   - *The New York Times*
David Richards   - *The New York Times*
Joel Siegel   - *WABC - TV*
John Simon   - *New York* magazine
Alisa Solomon   - *The Village Voice*
Edwin Wilson   - *Wall Street Journal*
Linda Winer   - *New York Newsday*

PLAYWRIGHTS/LYRICISTS, DIRECTORS, A COMPOSER AND AN ACTRESS:

Glenn Close   - actress

PREFACE

MY DREAM'S LONG JOURNEY TO REALITY

At age 27, all of a sudden I came by my first idol. The crucial discovery dawned on me one winter evening of 1989, when reading a Bulgarian cultural digest magazine, I came across an article from the Italian *Espresso* with a fearful title—*Frank—the Destroyer*—and with a not-in-the-least fearful photo of the destroyer in question. I read the article several times, almost not believing my eyes, then I tore out the two magazine pages, and they never left my desk in Bulgaria nor my purse in New York, until I finally met my idol in person.

Frank was Frank Rich—the first-string theater critic of *The New York Times*. He was called *"the Destroyer,"* because "with a single review he would make or break the most expensive Broadway extravaganzas;" because he had "taken up kind of a crusade against everything he would consider mediocre theater" and so on. The proofs for his deserving the sinister "title" were flowing one after another, but not a whiff of compassion for the supposedly "destroyed" was coming out of all that. The article was an echo of an obviously noisy New York theater skirmish, and a long quote from an indisputably accurate shot by Frank Rich served as a very powerful ending of the text. As a comment on the thoroughly convincing harangue of the *New York Times'* critic, the Italian author—Giovani Forti—had added only a phrase: "A devilish sophism, indeed!" That, together with the tone of the whole article, made me think that our admiration for the devil in question was equal. The only difference was that in my case it was not just admiration: described as he was, Frank Rich was, to me, a living embodiment of my as yet unrealized dream of the role theater criticism could play in the overall theater process.

I've always thought that applying high standards in criticism makes sense only if it has influence enough on its readership, so it could affect theater attendance; only in this case would theater artists have to take criticism into consideration, and therefore it could eventually affect the development of the whole theater process. In other words, influential criticism in the short run, to me, means improvement of theater in the long run.

At the time, in Bulgaria, the link between theater criticism and the readership was missing to the point that nobody cared what the critics were saying—neither the audience, nor the artists. Reviews were not in the least a factor for "whether to go to the theater" decisions. Getting favorable notices was a matter of prestige for the artists, but getting unfavorable ones didn't hurt the duration of the show's run at all. So it was kind of a "the dogs bark but the caravan goes on" situation. The main reasons for that were two: a) the criticism was out-dated in the sense that the reviews almost never appeared the week after the first night, let alone the next day; b) although knowledgeable, the criticism was not readable and interesting enough to capture the readers' attention. Everything that didn't meet the standards of the scientific-like "assessment—yes!, reporting—no!" pattern was looked down on as "pure journalism" and as writing too frivolous to be considered as serious criticism. It took me, for instance, several years of struggle with editors (Bulgarian periodicals don't have staff-critics) and a fluke to come across an editor who cared for the readership, rather than for the canon, so I could write my reviews in the not highly respected journalistic way. And, of course, I was able to only envy critics from countries where their reviews appeared the day after the premiere. The late coverage of the shows in my country made the reviews pointless, even if they were readable.

Briefly, whereas in the United States, as I was to find out later, criticism was called "a necessary evil", in Bulgaria it was not only "unnecessary," it was not even an "evil." Not that I wished it were so, but I believed (and I still do), that criticism can change theater for the better, provided it maintains high standards and provided it's influential enough to make these standards important to the audience and to the artists.

My dream of criticism's role in theater was so out-of-touch with reality that it seemed to be just wishful thinking—a mere abstraction. So when in 1989 I read the article about the *New York Times'* critic, I was amazed that there was a place on the earth where my abstraction was not an abstraction at all but a reality with a name—Frank Rich, who, at age of 41, had been calling the shots in the New York theater for the last ten years. Exactly a year later, Frank Rich was going to be staring curiously at his photo and the Cyrillic alphabet in the Bulgarian magazine. It was going to be his turn to be amazed by the expansion of his fame even to Bulgaria. Meanwhile, however, I had to arrange to meet him and I had a number of amazements ahead.

I stumbled over the first one right away. The day after I read the article, I went to the National Library in Sofia to read some of Frank Rich's reviews and I found out that there wasn't an issue of *The New York Times* available—the library simply didn't subscribe to it because of the cost. After a while I finally managed to get some of the paper's Sunday issues, but to my disappointment Frank Rich wasn't writing there. I was happy though to discover some quotes by him in the ads and in the theater directory. And by merely devouring everything about theater in the "Arts and Leisure" section, I got the exalted feeling of my dream's first touch to its distant reflection—the reality of New York theater criticism. I decided that I had to bring them together! So I wrote many letters to different American universities and foundations asking if I could do research on contemporary American theater criticism there, and I got many polite yes-but answers. Then, by a fluke, I found out about the Fulbright Fellowships and applied for one, and when I had almost given up hope, I got a "yes" answer. In two weeks I was to fly to the United States.

My dream was nearly bursting with curiosity when I brought it to New York at the end of September 1990. My dream's journey to reality had been accomplished geographically, but the real journey was still ahead. At first sight, not only was the reality overlapping my dream, it was overwhelming it. I was amazed by the bits of criticism that poured from everywhere: from posters on buses and in subway and railway stations, from theater directories, from ads in periodicals, on TV and on radio, from glittering theater marquees. I was able to hear the theater critics' names floating among the intermission crowds: "So and so said that show is wonderful—we should go see it!", or "It's no good—so and so said such and such!" My dream was jubilant, it couldn't believe its eyes that a critic could be such a celebrity! Three years before, just after my graduation with a degree in "Theater Arts and Criticism" from The Academy of Theater and Film Arts in Sofia, I had played the lead in the most successful Bulgarian movie and my popularity as an actress had helped to draw attention to my critical writing. So I could imagine what the "celebrity status" of the New York critics meant in terms of influence.

It was fascinating that I could read reviews the day or the week after the premiere. I relished the playful, conversational, and adventurous language of the reviews. I was enchanted by the skill of the critics in bringing out the experience and the spirit of the show, making it vivid, palpable, and vital. Of course, I was looking eagerly for every new piece by Frank Rich, but by that time, I already knew that he was not the only one. I wanted to meet these people—the powerful New York critics. I wanted to learn their professional secrets; I wanted to take a look at the New York theater criticism from inside.

I told my artistic advisers at New York University about my intention to conduct my research by interviewing the New York critics. The response was: "Forget it! Most of these people are inaccessible!" They were proven wrong: all the critics whom I've approached (with only one exception) agreed to meet with me and were very helpful.

Gradually, in the course of the interviews, embarrassment took over me: the picture of New York theater criticism, as described by its creators, looked quite different from my dream. For one thing, it was not all that rosy. So many problems and contradictions came up that I decided: instead of jumping at conclusions, I needed to see the other side of the picture. And I started doing interviews with producers, playwrights, directors, and press-agents.

As I met with more and more people, as I read more and more of and about New York theater criticism, as I saw more and more shows, I began discovering that a lot of the things which fascinated me so much were like double-edged weapons. My dream started finding its face sometimes distorted, as it was looking in the mirror of reality. I began to realize the paradoxes of New York theater criticism.

The first revelation was connected with the critics' "ad-celebrity-status." One day, I read a very negative review about a play, but in the next day's New York Times the ads ran a positive quote from that same review. To my astonishment, I found out that it's not against the law to distort the overall meaning of a critic's assessment, taking out of the review's context only words suitable for a rave ad! Obviously, there was a very fragile line between critics' celebrity-status and their criticism being boiled down to mere advertisement.

Next came the surprise that in many cases the reviews turned out to be more interesting, more moving, and even more imaginative, than the shows critiqued. And the greater the expectations for the show, based upon the critics' raves, the greater the disappointment in seeing the show itself. At one point I was close to the conclusion that New York criticism was much more interesting than New York theater. An exaggeration, of course, but not entirely! Now I think that if I were to put my opinion about the relationship between criticism and theater in New York in a single phrase, I would certainly not say: "much ado about nothing," but I wouldn't hesitate to say that it's not more than a "much ado about not a big something." And my guess is that the fault is mutual. On the one hand, when there aren't a lot of exciting things happening in the theater, it's obvious why the smallest sign of excitement is taken up by the critics and praised to the skies. On the other hand, however, I think that it's exactly the critics' job to keep standards high.

One more surprise came out of the comparison between actual theater productions and reviews. It became clear to me that praise and blame were sometimes passed out at random by critics. As if following a strict rule, the reviews customarily mention all the components of a show, with not a name omitted, but they don't always analyze them properly, if at all. That is especially noticeable on the rare occasions when the objects of criticism are classical plays or performances of guest European companies, let alone the combination, which puts many critics in an impasse. In other words, the highly readable critics' style is not always bolstered by a profound knowledge of the theater. My guess is that that phenomenon is a result of two major paradoxes of the American criticism, which I'd call: the "common-denominator" paradox and the "clean-hands" paradox.

The first one comprises one of the indisputably greatest assets of New York criticism—that, at its best, it provides the readers with a living and breathing impression of the show. Conveyed in an accessible, captivating, and very readable way, the critics' assessments naturally become of great importance to the readers. That, I think, is the aesthetic aspect of the overall explanation for the close interrelation between the New York critics and the audience. There is another side of the coin, however. It comes from the fact that the critiques are not just written exclusively *for* the audience, but are supposed to be written *from* the average theater goer's point of view. That common-denominator attitude of the critics, maintained as I was told in the name of the American journalistic tradition, can easily serve (and does serve) as a convenient way to avoid the need and the effort for more knowledge. The eager demonstration of fidelity to that unwritten rule can make professionals sound preposterous. In my interview with a leading New York critic, I was shocked to hear that that person tries to go to the theater with an open mind, not pretending to have any expert knowledge or experience. I didn't ask the critic: a) why having an "open mind" in the theater should be considered incompatible with having knowledge and experience, and b) why a connoisseur (which is what I think a critic should be) should try to pretend not to have knowledge and experience. It sounded and it still sounds too absurd and incomprehensible to me. Such an attitude,

I think, simply stultifies the critic's work. If a critic shouldn't be more than an ordinary member of the audience, then why should periodicals waste money for staff-critics? Instead, why not interview people from the public about their opinion on the shows?

The "common-denominator" paradox goes hand in hand with the "clean-hands" paradox. In my interviews, the questions which got almost unanimous "no" answers were: "Do you attend rehearsals?" and "Do you read the plays before reviewing them?" Another question with a nearly unanimous vote (in this case— yes) was: "Do you avoid being friends with theater people?" It's true that a lot of the critics with whom I've spoken have been involved with the theater before becoming critics, one way or another, but not necessarily in a way that brings an in-depth knowledge of it. From my own experience I know that from attending rehearsals (a mandatory part of our program) and from communicating with theater artists I have learned more about the theater than from anything else. I'm aware that that's at variance with the American journalistic tradition, and I'm far from putting myself in the ridiculous position to recommend that the New York critics follow a practice which is opposite to theirs. What I can say, though, as a two-year observer of their community, is that, in my opinion, the fear of being compromised by whatsoever involvement with the theater process results in an artificial self-isolation of the majority of the critics from the reality of the art they criticize. As if their professional positions and the fairness of their judgements could depend primarily on such "safety measures" and not on a critic's character, talent, knowledge, and skills. Critics are assiduous in preserving their objectivity, but at the same time there seems to be such a profusion and consequent devaluation of critics' enthusiasm: according to the ads critics are seeing "the best" this or that every other day. Can such enthusiasm be objective?

Something else: the critics' attempt to remain absolutely virgin outsiders in the art's temple and the hostility towards them on the part of the majority of the artists amounts to kind of "an iron curtain" between the two communities—certainly not to the profit of either of them. This is another absurdity to me!

"Community" is hardly the right word to describe all the New York theater critics put together. If there's anything lacking in their "society", it's a sense of community. No sooner had I entered the maze of their cultural milieu, than I was to discover that at times it felt like walking in a mine-field. The amount of feuding and the lack of tolerance is really amazing. But far more amazing is the ease with which some of the critics transfer their mutual antipathies to a third party. Actually losing someone's favour could be just a matter of mentioning not unfavorably the name of that person's enemy.

Towards the end of my research, I wrote an article describing the story of my coming and my stay in New York. Naturally, it began the same way as this foreword— with the Italian article about Frank Rich. I sent my story to several people. One of them, not long before, had made me a very interesting offer and had suggested that we should meet to discuss it thoroughly. When I called that person to set up an appointment the response was, "What do we have to talk about?" Stunned by such a question, I switched the conversation to my essay. There was another short and very irritated question, "Don't you know that here everybody hates Frank Rich?" As if the awareness of this fact could have changed the facts in my story! Later

I was very angry at myself that, shocked as I was, I didn't remind that person about another, quite opposite, statement by him: how flattered he had been when praised by Frank Rich as an example to emulate. Isn't that charming? (If I could take the liberty to use the expression with which Peter Shaffer concludes a similarly absurd story included in this book).

Most of the paradoxes I came across in New York theater and criticism were connected with the power-phenomenon. At first, I was dismayed that the critics' influence, which fascinated me so much, was something everybody was either opposing or denying. Then I understood that in fact critics didn't really wield that much influence over the artistic aspects of the theater. Maybe because, for the most part, criticism is more "audience competent" than artistically competent. Of course, there are also a whole cluster of other reasons. Next I came across the war against so-called "destructive criticism." Were the influential critics to follow the requirements of the patriots of this war, they should write only positive reviews in order to help theater survive. This is a paradox in itself, but the bigger paradox is that artists themselves would preach about the necessity for lowering critical standards. It's as if critics are viewed as members of a charity organization. Then I found out that the so much disputed critics' power was, to a great extent, a manipulatively mythological phenomenon, based on place of employment and mainly on economic factors. And that was the most dismal revelation to me.

I have a fantasy: what would happen if at one and the same time in Bulgaria the cost of theater productions and tickets should go sky-rocketing while on Broadway ticket prices would drop drastically? Would Bulgarian critics suddenly become crucially influential, whereas their New York colleagues would lose their power? Such a fantastic reversal, alas, would have nothing to do with the perfection of criticism itself.

Having said all that, I hear you asking me, whiff of sarcasm in your voice: "How's your dream doing now?" I still think that, at its best, American theater criticism is something worth dreaming about. But I also think that if it is combined with the best features of the European critics' style, nothing then could be compared to it! In other words, the disillusionments opened the eyes of my dream, and it came up with a new version of itself: a mixture of the European model and the American one at their best. Almost everybody in New York points to London, "Theater criticism over there is something of the kind," they say. Maybe my dream should take on a new journey and check up if that's true?

Kalina Stefanova-Peteva
New York, November 1992*

---

* This book is based on interviews conducted by me in New York and in Boston, in 1991 and in 1992. The excerpts included in the book have been revised and updated by my interviewees in September and in October 1992.

Part I
Confessions

1   25 WAYS TO
BECOME AN ORACLE:
THE NEW YORK THEATER CRITICS
TELL THEIR LIFE STORIES

Clive Barnes
Robert Brustein
Dennis Cunningham
Michael Feingold
Jeremy Gerard
Mel Gussow
William A. Henry III
Holly Hill
Jonathan Kalb
Stanley Kauffmann
Walter Kerr
Howard Kissel
Stewart Klein

Jack Kroll
Pia Lindstrom
Glenn Loney
Edith Oliver
Frank Rich
David Richards
Gordon Rogoff
Joel Siegel
John Simon
Alisa Solomon
Edwin Wilson
Linda Winer

They answer the questions:

- When, how, and why did you get interested in theater? Was that a continuation of a family tradition?

- When, how, and why did you make up your mind to become a theater critic?

- How has your career evolved through the years?

and more

CLIVE BARNES

I was born in London in 1927. My father was an ambulance driver and my mother was a secretary. I first became interested in theater around 1936. At that time my mother was working for a theatrical agency, for a very short time, but she did get free tickets. I remember the first musical I saw—*Me and My Girl,* I was nine then. I was ten when she took me to a revue—*Black and Blue.* In it there was a very good Jewish comedian, Max Wall, and in that revue I saw my first naked lady. About that time, from my school they took us to the Old Vic Theater. There I saw John Guilgud doing King Lear. I didn't understand it, but it made an incredible impression on me. In 1939 the war came; the school was evacuated out of London, but whenever I came back to town I went to the theater. I became obsessed with it.

At that time two other companies—the Sadler's Wells Ballet and the Sadler's Wells Opera—shared a theater with the Old Vic. So through the theater I became interested in ballet and opera, and in dance, too. I was 14 or 15 when I decided that I really wanted to write about theater and dance. It's very strange: almost all of the kids at that age want to become actors or dancers, but for me it never seemed a reasonable option. I had an awful stutter, I couldn't get a sentence without "Ah..ah..ah." And you couldn't have a stuttering Hamlet! I used to write poetry, but I had no creative ability. I also had no ambition: it never occurred to me to write a play. But I wanted to be part of the theater. So I conceived the idea of being a critic.

I won various scholarships for different schools and after making a false start as a medical student, and being for two years in the Royal Air Forces, I eventually went to Oxford—St. Catherine's College, where in 1951 I took my degree in English language and literature. By 1950 I was writing for the university newspaper. Kenneth Tynan was the theater critic, and I was the dance critic. In 1950 I also became an editor of a new magazine, *Dance and Dancers,* and I'm connected with that even today.

It was a difficult thing to get work in England in 1951. I started as a dance critic more than as a theater critic. First, I became dance critic for the *New Statesman* and *Nation.* In 1956 I became an assistant music critic for *The Daily Express.* I wrote also about movies and plays. In 1961 I became the chief dance critic of *The Times* of London. In 1963 I started writing as a free-lance for *The New York Times* from London about London, Europe, and so on.

In 1965 *The New York Times* was looking for a dance critic. There was no one really suitable for them of my age in America, so they invited me to come from London to be their dance critic. As soon as I got here, they started asking me to do drama as well, because they knew I had done drama in England: I'd been an executive editor of *Plays and Players.* But I didn't want to give up dance. English theater at that time particularly was much more interesting than the American theater, and American dance—just the opposite. So it hardly made any sense at all for an Englishman to come in America and cover American theater. In 1966 *The New York Herald Tribune* collapsed and the *Times* took Walter Kerr as a drama critic. He was extremely graceful, witty, and clever. Before then the drama critic had always written a daily review on the night and the Sunday review also. For the first time, they split the job up in 1966/67 season. I became the daily drama critic, and Walter Kerr was the Sunday critic. I also did dance—daily and the Sunday piece.

In 1977 I had a lot of trouble with the then-editor. He was obviously very anxious to get rid of me. At that time I happened to be rather well known, and thus a difficult person to dislodge. But anyway eventually he did it. He appointed somebody else as the drama critic, making me once more just the dance critic. Rupert Murdoch had asked me, sometime before, to go to the *New York Post*, because he was trying to change it and he had offered me a fabulous salary—at least twice what I was being paid at the *Times*. I was tempted, but not really that tempted. But when I was more or less fired by the *Times*, I was very angry. By that time I was doing both drama and dance, and I enjoyed it, and I felt it would be very unjust to American drama just to say, "Well, I'm not interested!" They wanted me to write. So I went to Murdoch and said, "You offered me a job. Are you still interested?" And we negotiated. He didn't give me quite the salary that he had offered previously. But it was not really the money. I just wanted to continue to write about theater. So in 1977 I went to the *New York Post* to do both dance and drama.

- What did you lose leaving the *Times*? What's the feeling of losing power particularly?

Clive Barnes: I didn't mind losing power. What you do lose is public visibility. I don't miss that very much. Our audience at the *New York Post* is a very good one. Personally, I don't think I've lost that much. A lot of prestige, of course, but that never worried me.

- What did you gain?

Clive Barnes: I'm given a lot more freedom at the *New York Post*. Now we are cutting back a lot of space and you don't have the same freedom, but until a year ago, I had an absolute freedom. Here I gained a complete authority of my copy.

- You mean you didn't have it before?

Clive Barnes: At the *Times* there are always pressures. When I was a critic there, all the editors used to go to the first night. Also, they had a very strong idea about what wasn't proper for the *Times*. They wouldn't use the first person singular. I was the first person on *The New York Times* to use that. I feel it very important that people understand that there is no objectivity in criticism, that it's merely someone offering an informed but subjective opinion. Therefore, the use of "I" is not egoistical. It's simply a reminder to the reader that this is one person's opinion and that it's perfectly valid to disagree. One of the disadvantages of the way Americans read criticism is that there is a concept of the judgmental qualities of criticism. As a matter of fact, the good critic is not a judge but an advocate, he's expressing a view about the theater, arguing for that view.

ROBERT BRUSTEIN

- Your way of becoming a theater critic, as you describe it in your book *The Third Theater*—"I thought it would help me get practical work in the theater."— is more than unusual. You've said that your friend Elliot Silverstein has told

you that when you reach a certain level of prominence as a critic then you can direct, act, do anything you want. Now, when you've really got all that, what do you think of your friend's advice?

Robert Brustein: I haven't thought about that for a long time, but it seems kind of absurd now. I hope it's not just because I've reached a certain level as a critic, that I've been functioning as a practical theater person for the last 25 years. I didn't think it was accurate advice. I certainly had reached some sort of a dead end functioning in the practical theater at the time. I was very unsatisfied with the plays, directors, and people I was meeting, and I thought: I want to give up this thing. As a result I went into academic life and started a doctorate in Dramatic Literature, and I also began practicing criticism. It was only after I was offered the job at Yale that it began to occur to me that I might have some impact on the very things that so dissatisfied me when I was working as an actor.

- You've begun writing criticism in order to get into practice. But you haven't given it up after you've reached your goal. Why?

Robert Brustein: I enjoy writing. It's one of the few things, in fact the only one, that I do by myself. Everything else I do in collaboration with others. It's a form of sublimation when you subordinate your own needs and your own vanity to the needs of others—you work through them and you get your satisfaction through watching them develop. But occasionally I need satisfactions of my own and I get these through writing. So that's why I don't give up writing.

- Is this the only reason you continue writing criticism?

Robert Brustein: No. I do it also because it gives me an opportunity to see plays outside of my own theater which I normally might not have the energy to go to. It makes me think about what I believe in and it keeps me fresh. It gives me new ideas about how to run my own theater.

DENNIS CUNNINGHAM

I'm from a New Jersey working–class family. Nobody was in the theater. In high school I was interested in movies and it took me a couple of years to get to the live theater. I became fascinated by it and I got into it: I even directed for a while, but mostly I acted. I'm still in Actors Equity. I went to the Ph.D. theater program of Carnegie—Mellon University in Pittsburgh. Then I was teaching and acting ocasionally for TV, and someone said, "They need a reviewer at CBS TV station in Philadelphia. Why don't you audition?" I said, "O.K.", and I didn't care, I mean, I had no interest in it at all. That's how I got the job: I probably gave a great audition because I didn't want the job. Actually I was a tenured associate professor in college and I had to give that up, and I said, "I'll try TV, because this way you can really teach hundreds of thousands of people, hopefully, without looking as if you're teaching."

In the 1978 I came to New York, and I've been here ever since.

MICHAEL FEINGOLD

I've always been interested in the theater. It isn't particularly a family tradition, although my family—East European in origin—was always fond of theater, music, and art, and that was a natural part of our life. My mother was a musician by training. She was a piano teacher in Chicago, so I grew up with classical music in the house.

I didn't expect to make my life in the theater. What happened was: I came to New York to go to college at Columbia University. While I was in school I was studying French and I went to see Jean Louis Barrault's company, performing four different plays in four different styles on four successive nights; that was an experience that impressed me tremendously. This was a period when it was much cheaper to go to the theater in New York, and there was a very steady large group of people who went to plays much more often than now; the Broadway play was the common theatrical currency of American culture. This was about 30 years ago. So I grew up in a different context from the one younger people have now; it never occurred to me that there was a disparity between popular theater and taking the theater seriously.

My most influential teacher at Columbia University was Robert Brustein, and it happened by coincidence that, having decided to make a career in theater, I applied to the Yale School of Drama to study playwriting just at the time that he became the Dean of that school. I spent the next ten years at Yale: as a student, then as Bob's teaching-assistant, then as the first dramaturg of the Yale Repertory Company. At the same time I was one of the three founding editors of *Yale/Theater* magazine, and I also started to work at *The Village Voice,* as a free-lance and then as a regular critic. So I've spent half of my adult working life in the theater—as a translator, a playwright, a literary manager, and a dozen other odd jobs. I became a working theater artist at the same time that I became a critic. Part of the latter was due to Robert Brustein, who thought that I was not cut out to be a playwright. When I was an undergraduate, he said to me, "You should be a critic!" Later, I must say, he was the one who gave me my first opportunities for playwriting—writing children's shows and adapting Brecht's *Happy End* for the Yale Rep.

JEREMY GERARD

I have attended the theater all my life. It was part of the tradition in my family and by the time I was eight or nine years old I was going to the theater regularly. In high school and in college I was involved in theater productions as a director, as an actor, and occasionally as a writer. In college I made a switch from wanting to be in the theater to wanting to be a journalist and particularly a critic, because I had the opportunity to study with some very fine literary and theater critics. The key ones were Julius Novick and George Levine. Then I learned by doing it. First, I wrote for a very small community publication, then for bigger ones, then I left New York for several years. My first daily newspaper job was in Dallas at *The Dallas Morning News*—I was their theater critic for three years. Then I came back to New York and I was the chief theater reporter at *The New York Times* for a couple of years. Then I began reporting on other things for them until I came to *Variety,* in January 1991, as a theater editor and chief theater critic.

While I was doing this other political and critical work at the *Globe,* I continued to be involved in theater. I did some occasional theater reviewing and in my TV writings I often dealt with the relationship between TV and more traditional culture, particularly theater and dance. I was also the chairman of the board of a theater company in Boston, at which I appeared as an actor occasionally, and I wrote some performance pieces for the troupe. I also did a little bit of stage directing. With some friends, I did *Who's Afraid of Virginia Wolf?,* directing it and playing George. Since then I haven't done any acting, because it's not possible with my schedule and it's not appropriate for a major critic to be an actor as well. Nobody would take you seriously in either role, and there are so many potential conflicts of interest. But having had the practical experience of doing theater work makes me much more knowledgeable as a critic. Some other critics have had the practical experience as well, but a great many haven't and it shows. They complain about the absence of things that aren't possible to achieve, or about the play one didn't write. They never know which creative artist to credit or blame for what. One reason I know that this practical experience is valuable in criticism is from the Bob Fosse documentary show that I made for PBS network, which brought me the Emmy Award for the best informational special of the year. I had been reviewing documentaries arrogantly for a decade and more with barely a clue of how they are put together. I learned a great deal, including some humility, while making that show. Today I'm certainly more compassionate and better as a TV critic.

After the Pulitzer Prize, I got several job offers, among them from *Time* and the *New York Daily News*. The offer from the *Daily News* was for more money and to write as a critic at large, so the boss at *Time* said to me, "You'd probably regret not taking it. That experiment of theirs probably is not going to work. (The *Daily News* was launching a new paper and trying to change its basic audience.) But it'll be the most watched thing in American journalism and you should be part of it, and if you don't come here now, the door is open for you later." I went to the *Daily News*. But it quickly became apparent to me that it was the worst run place I'd ever seen and after seven months I moved on to *Time*. The first year I was based in the Nation section, doing political news but borrowed about half the time by various show-business sections to write pieces for them. 10 months later, I became the press critic. Not long afterwards I got a very attractive offer from *The Boston Globe* to become the managing editor of the Sunday paper, and to have at the same time a column. But I decided to stay at *Time* because they promised I would become their theater critic, which I did at the beginning of 1985.

HOLLY HILL

Being an actress helped me to express directly my love for the theater. I got to play some wonderful roles in a variety of classics and modern plays—from youngsters to the 95-year-old woman in *The Chairs*. What I found out about myself as an actress was that I was nothing special. I occasionally gave performances, which I as a critic might have said were really good—like Anne Frank. My best talent actually was for comedy, but I wasn't anywhere nearly as good as Meryl Streep, and I wasn't even in the same class as some of the fine actresses that we have. But it was a wonderful experience and preparation for being a critic, because I also was in various plays, where I did backstage work.

I quite deliberately decided to be a university professor as my basic living and to have theater criticism in addition. Being a theater critic really is a privileged life—to have two free tickets for all Broadway shows and to be on the first-night list—it's glamorous in its own way. On the other hand, teaching in the City College students from predominantly poor neighborhoods and backgrounds that have nothing to do with theater gives me a sense of reality. I remember taking one of my favorite students—a woman at 35 with five children, who is now a lawyer—as a graduation present to dinner and theater. She had never been to a French restaurant and to a Broadway show before that. It was one of the most magical nights in her life, but it was just another night in the theater to me. Having her ecstasy as a reference point is very valuable to me. Whenever I feel a bit jaded and burnt out I try to remember that. It helps a lot because burning out is a constant danger for a critic.

The first year that I was the Off-Broadway critic for the *Westchester/Rockland Newspapers* I really thought I was going to die. I had wanted to be a theater critic very much and I had done some spot criticism, but this was the first time, that I had ever gone to maybe a 100 plays in one year and written a lot. I had never before realized the amount of mediocre plays the critic sees and how deadly boring the job could be. There were weeks when I thought I never wanted to see another play. I thought, "What made me want to do this terrible job?!" But then I was asked to write a year-end round-up of the reviews of everything that I had seen and I realized that all of the mediocre things were pretty much forgotten. What I tended to remember were either the real disasters, but most of all—the really wonderful performances or plays. And I said, "That's what I'm going to carry with me for the rest of my life."

JONATHAN KALB

Although no one else in my family would recognize or name it as such, I think of myself as coming from a theater family. It was certainly a theatrical family. I was surrounded by a certain histrionism, or histrionic behavior, from the beginning, which made me grow up thinking that exaggeration for the sake of effect was necessary and normal part of life.

In school I went through all the typical experiences of a typical suburban kid interested in the theater—acting in school plays and so on. And in college I wrote four plays and directed them myself. I still sometimes think of myself as a playwright caught in the middle of an extended hiatus from playwriting enforced by the specter of Samuel Beckett.

My first experience as a theater critic was an internship at *The Middletown Press* in Connecticut. That was an extraordinary formative experience. It gave me a real taste of what it means actually to work in a newspaper and write on a deadline. It gave me the chance to become familiar with a body of theater work in a particular geographical area, because I had a sort of "beat": Hartford Stage, Yale Rep, and

Long Wharf Theater. Frankly, my primary reason for doing this was that I wanted the free tickets. I liked to write but I'd be lying if I said that I had any value for theater criticism as such at that point.

Then I moved to New York and worked in the literary office of Circle Repertory Theater—full-time for $50 dollars a week. That was a sobering reminder of the earning potential of my bachelor's degree, at least if I wanted to work in the arts, but it was also an experience that convinced me I needed a more solid background in dramatic literature and theater history. I wasn't satisfied with the level at which I was commenting on plays in my reports for the theater (which my superiors were perfectly happy with). And I started to read performance and literary theory on my own. The following year I enrolled in the Dramaturgy and Dramatic Criticism Program at the Yale School of Drama, and that turned out to be the perfect thing for me, largely because Yale has a theater magazine and that was a place to write for. I must say, getting a doctorate is in many ways exactly the wrong preparation for the job of theater critic, but I couldn't see that back then.

After Yale I went to Berlin on a Fulbright grant and finished my book on Becket there. Upon returning, I wrote a letter to Erica Munk, then theater editor of *The Village Voice,* and I enclosed a collection of my articles. She liked them, called me, and said, "Let's try." Her question about me was whether I could work under time pressure, so she gave me a play to see and asked for the review the next day. She liked the piece, and after that she called me regularly to write for the theater section. I was and am much more uncertain about my tolerance of space pressure.

If you ask me, "What do you do?", though, I'd probably answer, "I am a writer," not "I'm a theater critic." I write other things—essays, plays, poetry—and I'd like people to think I'm an interesting writer, not a trusty consumer guide. The problem is that very few people in America are prepared to pay a serious writer to write exactly what he wants to write. There's a sentence Stanley Kauffmann likes to repeat to his students, "If you want to be a serious writer in America, you have to have another source of income!" That's why I became a professor.

STANLEY KAUFFMANN

I became interested in the theater when I was a boy at school: I was in plays and I wrote plays. When it came time for university, I thought I was going to be a doctor, because my father was a dentist. I actually went to the university and registered to be a pre-med one day, but then I said, "No, I don't really want to do this. I want to be in the theater." It was in the depths of the Depression—in 1931, and one of the most silly things economically was to be in the theater, so I was very surprised when my parents agreed. I went to New York University and entered what was called the Department of Dramatic Art. I studied dramatic literature and some directing, but I was mostly concerned with acting. There was a repertory company connected with this department, that specialized mostly in Shakespeare. It was called *The Washington Square Players*—not the group that's in the history books, but a different one. It played in Greenwich Village, in two theaters at New York University. I stayed with that company long after I finished the university—

a total of 10 years. I played small parts; I was not a leading actor of the company by any means, but I did a lot of stage managing, lighting, music, and I thought I was going to spend my life there. We did a lot of things including a play by me. The company broke up in 1941 for various reasons including the war. I did other things then: I did a lot of writing, published novels. I had various positions— in editing, in magazines, in book publishing; I directed in radio and a little in the theater.

I came into writing criticism more or less by accident: a friend of mine, who was on a magazine in the '50s asked me to begin reviewing records of plays. I'd never done any criticism before and I liked it, and at the end of that decade the chance came for me to be a film critic: first for *The Reporter,* then in 1958 for *The New Republic,* which I'm still with. In the early '60s PBS-TV asked me to do a film series, which I did once a week, and then they asked me to be on another program doing theater criticism at the same time. Then it so happened that there came a vacancy at *The New York Times* and, through my TV work and their reading of my various articles on other subjects, they offered me the job. It was in late 1965. I stayed 8 months only—till August 1966. I was at odds with the people there, and I went back to *The New Republic*—first as a literary critic, then as a film and theater critic. From 1969 to 1979, I did both of them: three weeks I did films, one week—theater. In 1979, the theater critic they had before me—Robert Brustein— came back, so I continued with film criticism and I moved to a different magazine— *The Saturday Review,* to write theater criticism, and I kept that up for five or six years till the magazine died. Since then I've been writing only film criticism regularly. I've kept on writing articles on drama from time to time, but I haven't been regularly reviewing plays since about 1985.

My first regular teaching began at the Yale School of Drama in 1967. I stayed there with a few variations until 1986. About 1977 I began teaching also in the Graduate Center of City University of New York—till now.* That's my sad story.

WALTER KERR

The other evening I went to see *Cinema Paradiso.* That's my life story. The truth is that I made exactly that kind of friendship with the projectionist in my own town when I was about eleven or twelve years old. The censor came in twice a week to change the bill. She would sit down and look at the film and take her notes, and I would be watching through one of these holes at the back, so I saw everything she cut. The projectionist, who was supposed to restore that cut material and send it on, was throwing it away. I asked him, "May I have it?" And he said, "Sure!" So I made a collection of this material. Now, I was both shocked and stunned to see this in *Cinema Paradiso,* and at the same time I thought, "Well, this could happen any time."

My birth town was a small one of about 70,000 people. My mother was of great

---

* Stanley Kauffmann left CUNY in June 1992 and now teaches at Adelphi University.

help to me. She could see how much I cared about films, so from the time I was about six or seven years old she would take me to the movie houses and she would say, "Do you have any film you don't need anymore, that you can give to that little boy?" And they'd give me something, maybe a Fox newsreel. I had one of these kiddies' machines—I would put the projector on the kitchen stove and point it at the wall to see the image.

I didn't really become sure that I wanted to switch to the theater all through high school. I was in a process of a slow switch. I could go downtown Chicago where there were still 12, 13 legitimate theaters. My best friend was a high school actor, and he was always urging me, "Come on down, see this thing, it's great!" Films were silent up to now. It was the new thing—sound and voice—which won me over. I could see that speech was deeper: you get more psychology out through speech, than through faces.

Gradually I got beyond the kid reviewing that I'd been doing till then (a column about kids by a kid). I wasn't a kid anymore so I told my editor, "Let me do something on film, even if it's just news bits." He said, "O.K. Let's try!" At the same time with my friend we started writing plays to see if we could do it.

After college I taught for ten years. During that time we did five or six Broadway shows. My wife and I collaborated on several.

In 1950 I took a year off. One day I was sitting in the dining room in our house, in Washington, and I was looking at two piles of paper. One was a tall stack, the other—short and skimpy. We had a show running on Broadway and it had been quite successful, thank God, because we had a lot of flops along the way. I'd also written an article for the Sunday *New York Times,* which was reprinted in a lot of newspapers and I got a great deal of mail on it. The first pile, the big one, had to do with the article, and the second one—the skimpy one, was about the show. What the piles were telling me was obvious. I mean, here I am, I did all this work on the show: I worked on the lyrics, on the book, I directed the show, and this other thing is the one that catches readers' attention. Somehow I worked better on a critical level, so I said, "O.K., I'm going to try the other way around."

At that point, almost fortuitously, a job opened up at *Commonweal* magazine. I saw a note that their critic was leaving, so I wrote a message. Within a month they said, "Sure!" Some people tell me that it was the best thing I've ever done. By the time my second year at that magazine started, I was also on the *Herald Tribune.* And that was a matter of: I'm getting up to read the papers at breakfast one morning and I see that *The* New *York Herald Tribune* doesn't have a critic. So I went there and I was there for 15 years.

Brooks Atkinson was working on *The New York Times* during the first half of my period at the *Herald Tribune.* He was a wonderful man. We had standing dinner invitations at least once a month. It was a rule. It was a very special sort of situation, because we were trying neck-to-neck to beat each other out for the fun of it. It was like, oh God, an exhilarating game of what's your favorite sport.

- I wouldn't be surprised if you said that on the very same day the *Herald Tribune* went out of business you found out that the *Times* was looking for a drama critic.

Walter Kerr: I knew it anyway, because somebody had called me on the phone earlier, without saying anything in particular, using a very guarded double talk, but in fact inviting me over to join the *Times*. I told him, "I admire the *Times* and I thank you for asking me, but the *Herald Tribune* is in a lot of trouble. It gave me my chance in New York, so I can not walk out like that." I heard later that the next day my informant called the owner of the *Herald Tribune* and said, "You, sure, have very loyal staff over there." When the *Herald Tribune* closed, I went to the *Times* with the agreement that I could be only the Sunday critic except for the first year, because they wanted time to find a new daily critic. I didn't really like that situation but I did it, because they requested.

- Having experienced so many fortuitous things in your life, do you believe in luck?

Walter Kerr: I don't think about it. But, yes, I consider myself very, very lucky. I remember when I was just starting these kid reviews way back, they gave me an office, so I got the editing done there. One day the boss came across to me with a piece of paper in his hand and told me, "Take a look at that!" It was a letter from him "To Whom It May Concern," and it was recommending me very highly. But I hadn't asked him for anything! The world is full of good people. I've found out that at every step along the way there was somebody who helped me.

- Which period of your life do you consider the happiest one?

Walter Kerr: The first time that I was really deliriously happy with the way things were going was when I got back to school. The Depression was relentless: we had to sell out, give up the house, everything, I couldn't go to school; there was no money even for the superficial things. I tried but wasn't getting a job and then I decided to sit down and write to all the film exchanges in Chicago, and eventually I worked for Fox films for a year and a half. After that I still didn't have enough money for school, so I went to the dean of the school and I said, "Can you give me some work to do that would pay my tuition?" And we talked for a while and he ended up saying, "Yes!", and he gave me the next three years of my school life.

Another happy period was all my time in Washington, the years while I was teaching at Catholic University. I stopped one day to think about it: all of that spread of eleven years seemed to me a vacation. It was all fun; it was all play. I wasn't fighting for a place on Broadway, which is much harder—that's work, or criticism— criticism is work, the way we did it.

HOWARD KISSEL

I agree with Moss Hart, who wrote that the theater is the refuge of the unhappy child. I don't think you take up theater the way you do collecting stamps or building model airplanes. I realized at a certain age—not more than seven or eight—that I was fascinated by the theater, that I loved reading plays, that I loved to act.

We used to do plays in grade school. It was the happiest time for me. In high school and in college I continued acting and writing. While I was in high school, back in Milwaukee, I went once a month to see the touring companies of Broadway shows. Within four years I saw such things as Julie Harris in *The Lark,* Miriam Hopkins in *Look Homeward, Angel,* Rip Torn and Geraldine Page in *Sweet Bird of Youth,* directed by Elia Kazan, and the Lunts in *The Visit,* directed by Peter Brook. Those productions shaped my understanding of what theater was and filled me with a tremendous enthusiasm for it.

I really wanted to be an actor, but, when I came to New York "to seek my fortune" in 1967, I realized that the kind of theater I wanted to do—classical theater—virtually no one was doing. Twenty years later that is still true.

I majored in English and Comparative Literature at Columbia University and received a Master's in Journalism from Northwestern.

My first job was writing about men's fashion for Fairchild Publications, which put out a number of fashion publications, including the chic *Women's Wear Daily.* At that time *WWD* was very influential. They not only wrote about what Seventh Avenue garment manufacturers were making and what was being shown in Paris, but they were smart enough to realize that you can't write about fashion in a vacuum. They also wrote about fashionable society and the way it intersected with politics and the arts.

In 1970 *Women's Wear* instituted a page of reviews of arts, to which anyone who worked for the company was allowed to contribute. I began by doing book reviews and second string movie reviews. I did, however, enjoy writing about men's fashions, which was my job at Fairchild, so, in 1971, I took a position writing features for *GQ (Gentlemen Quarterly).*

Four months later I was offered the editorship of the arts page of *Women's Wear,* which I took. In 1972 the film critic left, so I became the film critic. In 1974 the theater critic left, so I also became the theater critic. I stayed there until 1986, when I was offered the job of theater critic at *The Daily News.*

STEWART KLEIN

I was born in Philadelphia and I grew up dreaming of coming to New York; seeing Broadway opening nights, films, night clubs, heavy-weight championship fights, and all of it. I've always loved the theater and I love films, and that's what I wanted to do. Unfortunately, in America you just do not go to school and get a job as a critic. So I went to college, Temple University, and majored in journalism. At the same time, for four years I worked as a copy-boy for *The Philadelphia Inquirer,* and when I got out of college I went to work as a reporter for *The Philadelphia Daily News.* I later worked for CBS News and ABC News, and for a radio station in New York—as a reporter, news-editor, and news-writer. I worked in "hard" news for ten years before I got my first chance to do a review.

It was funny: the man who was our regular theater reviewer was on a vacation and the boss came out, and said, "Who would like to do a review tonight of a Broadway play?" And I raised my hand, and that night I was very good. And the boss said, "You keep on doing it!" While I was doing the reviews, I was working full-time as a reporter, covering political speeches, fires, murders, labor strikes. And I would go to the theater at night, not getting paid for it, just because I loved it.

I did that on radio for several years, and then Channel 5 started a news program, and they offered me a job as critic. This was 1967, and I've been there ever since, which is very unusual; people on TV usually do not last very long: every year or so somebody who's young and has blond hair, and good teeth gets hired, and the older people get fired. But I managed to hang on for a long time and I suppose I'm now the senior TV critic in New York City.

JACK KROLL

I was always caring about the arts more than anything else. I started to write when I was just a child. I was nine, ten years old, I used to go to the movies, I came back home and wrote about it—just for me. Where it comes from? I don't know. My father was a very interesting guy. He divorced my mother when I was five years old and then he became a very famous radio personality. My mother was a show-girl; she was on Broadway as a dancer.

I majored in English literature at City College in New York. Then I went into the Army—this was in the Korean war. When I came back I taught English for a while at Hunter College, but I decided that the academic life was not for me. I was offered a job by an advertising agency and I did that for several years. Meanwhile I started writing reviews for various magazines as a free-lance. This was the time of the New York School of the Abstract-Expressionist painters and *Art News* magazine was their spokesman. There was a very famous editor at that magazine—Thomas Hess. He had seen my writing so he called me and asked me to work for them writing about art. It was the most exciting period there's ever been in this country, as far as art is concerned; Abstract Expressionism, Pop Art—all these things were just exploding. I covered that stuff for *Art News* for several years. Then I got married and I needed more money.

Meanwhile *Time* magazine had done a piece about me as sort of a new voice in art criticism, and the person who wrote the article said, "If you ever want to change the job come to work for us." After I got married, I remembered that. I called them and I told my editor that I was going to go there because I needed more money. He understood that but said, "Don't do that." I asked him, "Why?" He said, "If you want to go to that business, you should go to *Newsweek*" I said, "But *Newsweek* is just a second-rate version of *Time*!" "Yes," he said. "That's the way it has been up to now, but from now on they are going to be the most exciting place, because a few new people are going to be there and they are going to do a lot of new things."

So in 1964, I came over to *Newsweek* and he was right. I was hired as the art critic. About a year later the editors created an art section, equal with all the other parts of the magazine, which had never been done in *Newsweek* before. I became an editor of that section. At that time both in *Time* and in *Newsweek* there were no by-lines. When I became an editor, I put on by-lines for the first time. That totally changed the business. Four years later, *Time* did the same thing. I was writing about the arts, books, ballet, music, theater, movies. About twelve years later, there came a new bunch of editors; they changed everything around, and I started focusing on theater and film. Occasionally I still do a piece about art, music, or books. I've been there for all these years now.

From the very beginning, I was mostly attracted by the idea of writing about high culture for the mass audience. It was so exciting to find a new language to do that. And I was lucky with my editor in *Art News* who let me experiment. He would tell me that people would come to him and would say, "Tom, Jack is a wonderful guy, but why do you let him write these pieces?" And he would say, "Because I understand what he's trying to do." Then I was very lucky with my editors in *Newsweek*.

PIA LINDSTROM

I didn't really "make up my mind" to become a critic. About 15 years ago the job of the theater critic opened and a friend, Robert Anderson, the playwright, said, "Why don't you audition for it. You know enough." And I said: "O.K. I'll try." Eventually I got the job. I had been a reporter for ten years. I've been at WNBC-TV, for almost 20 years, and I worked for WCBS-TV for three years before that—always as a reporter. The skills you use covering a news story, or a fire, or a press-conference, or a murder are the same. The only difference is that now I give an opinion. In the past I didn't say, "It was a good fire or a bad fire." I simply said, "It was a fire," and let somebody else say how long it was going to take to put it out.

Because of the time constraint, one has to be very careful not to be too clever— you don't have time for that. It's a constant problem of eliminating and selecting what you are going to leave out and what you are going to put in. You are making judgements even down to things like adjectives. You need just say what you thought of it and I've discovered that the first idea is always the right one. When you walk out of a movie and somebody asks you, "What do you think of it?"—that's what you really think of it. If you go back and try to fix it up, and make it sound better, because you want to seem more clever, you destroy the spontaneity. And because I don't have time to make allusions to the history of the theater, someone might argue that it's a disservice to the theater or to films, or to the artists, and a good argument could be made that it is, but I can't help that. I work for a TV company, and that's what they want from me. If I did it differently I'd lose my job. My children are at school, I can't afford losing my job! I regret that I'm not given a 100 minutes to discuss things, but I'm not—that's a fact of life.

When I began I used to be so nervous. I'd always go to the lobby and try to listen to everybody else because I was afraid I was wrong. I've had those terrible experiences when I'm the only one who likes something everybody else hates, or I hated it and everybody else loved it. I also used to get up in the morning and read Frank Rich, and he'd said the opposite to what I'd said and I thought he must be right and I must be wrong, because he's in *The New York Times*. But after a while I started to realize that it doesn't matter, because there can not be a "right" or a "wrong" opinion. It's just an opinion and it's very personal.

GLENN LONEY

I grew up in a very fundamental protestant family. None of them had ever been to the theater. They knew it was the trap of the devil, and all the people who work in the theater become whores and drunks. But I went to a wonderful school in California: all 8 grades in one room. Every Friday, all the farmers would come and their wives would bring cakes, and we were expected to sing some songs or do recitations. So I'd write plays, not very good ones, because I didn't know how to write a play. In high school, we did a little bit of drama. Then I went to college. I was going to be a civil engineer, because my father had such a dream. But when I went to the University of California at Berkeley to enroll, I saw: for engineering you have to pay $25 for laboratory fees, $25 for physics, and for chemistry $25. And I had to pay my own way. $75? And I really don't like math! The rules were that at Berkeley everybody had to take at least one language and one science, and looking around I saw: botany $2.50, and at that moment I was no longer a civil engineer, I was a humanities student. I found a very interesting major—"Speech"; each of the professors was an expert in something having nothing to do with speech: a sociologist, a historian, a famous artist, a lawyer. So it was a whole humanities education, with the unifying thing that we wrote speeches and we got up and we spoke about important topics. I was also working on the student newspaper, so I started taking journalism. Then I started working on the lights in the University Theater. And you ought to be in a play; you ought to direct a play; you ought to design a play. So when I ended up, I had a "group major": journalism, English, theater, and speech, which was the best training I ever could have. Except when I graduated, I asked myself: What am I good for? I'm only good to teach! I went to Stanford and I got my doctorate there. No sooner had I finished the dissertation, than I was drafted into the army. When I got out of the army, I went to San Francisco State College to ask for a job. The secretary was telling me that there wasn't even one course when the phone rang from the hospital that one of the professors had been hit by a streetcar. So they gave me her courses but not as a regular job. I thought I had to do something better than this. I was interviewed by the University of Nevada and they said, "We are starting a campus in Las Vegas," so I went there and I was teaching English and theater in Las Vegas, if you can imagine!

Then I went to Europe for four years with a rank of a full professor. It was a lovely time to be there. I went to the theater a lot. But I thought: I don't have a regular job with tenure; there's no future here for me, so I have to go back to America. I got off the plane with no job again, but I'd had the good fortune stopping off in England to stumble into a Speech and Theater Conference, and there were some people from Hofstra University on Long Island. They hired me, and I worked there for two years and then I went to Brooklyn College, where I've been ever since.

EDITH OLIVER

I'm a New Yorker. My parents were just private people who loved the theater. So I've been going to the theater since I was five years old. When I was in high school, on Wednesday afternoons, I'd rush to the subway, leave my coat, mingle with the intermission crowds, and sneak into the theater. Then when I was eighteen, I went to a summer theater and I saw Act 1 of all the plays that I'd sneaked into in the intermissions, because all I'd seen then was Act 2 or Act 3. So I always liked the theater and thought all the ushers were fooled.

When William Shawn, my editor, asked me to work at *The New Yorker,* I said, "I would love to, if I never have to write anything!", and he said, "I promise." I was hired as his assistant: I saw writers for him, I read manuscripts. Then I was handed the Book Review department, which I still run. I think of that as my job. The theater is my fun. Then one year we were changing jobs. The movie job was open, and the editor said, "Raise your hands, who wants to do it!" And do you know what I said? I said, "You, son of a bitch, how long do I have to make up my mind?" And he said, "20 seconds." So I said, "Yes." I started to do movies every summer when the regular movie critic was on a vacation, and then he gave me Off-Broadway, so I did it for many years. My first Off-Broadway review was, I think, in 1962. Several years ago I became the main theater critic.

FRANK RICH

I fell in love with the theater the minute that I saw it, when I was first taken to the theater by my parents. As a child I wanted to be an actor, a director, a set designer. My parents have nothing to do with the theater. My father had a shoe-store and used to bring me home empty boxes, and I'd see plays and build the sets in them.

I'm from Washington, D.C. Then it was a very big news center. I was always interested in theater and in newspapers. And as time went on, theater criticism presented itself to me as a way of merging those two interests. But while I never seriously thought about pursuing a career in the theater, I've always been interested in journalism. I started writing reviews when I went to college. At Harvard, at that time there was no such a thing as theater or journalism major, so I majored in American history and literature. *The Harvard Crimson* was one of the best student newspapers and I auditioned to be a writer there. I wrote drama and film reviews. When I graduated from Harvard, I got a fellowship to go to Europe and travel: I went to England and I saw a lot of theater, and to France, Israel, and the Far East.

As a graduate I sold my first articles, which were about politics. I had been at Harvard during the late '60s, during the Vietnam war and the students' upheavals. There was a huge story then, as big as the Watergate scandal for its time, about some secret papers connected with the Vietnam war, which were leaked by a man, Daniel Ellsberg, whom I knew, to *The New York Times*. He was arrested, and I did a profile about him for *Esquire,* and that started me as a journalist. Then, with some friends from college, we started a weekly newspaper in Richmond—a kind of political newspaper, like *The Boston Phoenix*—and I covered politics and the arts. Because of my writing for *Esquire* and because of that paper I came to the attention of someone who was starting a new magazine in New York—*New Times;* I was hired as a film critic and an editor, and I moved to New York. That was 1973. In 1975, the *New York Post* contacted me and I became their first-string film critic. After three years, they decided to make it into a sensational tabloid and I quit it. A few months later, I was hired by *Time* magazine; I was a film and TV critic for it from 1977 to 1980, when *The New York Times* was looking for a new drama critic and I was recruited by them.

- **Without being a drama critic before?**

Frank Rich: Not professionally. What happened was: I had always wanted to be a drama critic. My first love was theater. Films were not my great passion, while theater was. So I really waited around. When I came here, they gave me a six-month try-out, I succeeded, and they promoted me to the job, which I have to this day.

- **Could you point out the main changes you've gone through as a theater critic at *The New York Times?***

Frank Rich: I just hope I've become a better writer. The theater has gone through a lot of stages. I've gone through a lot of stages in my own life. It's hard for me to really look at how I've changed over 12 years. It's up to the reader to judge. I've always tried to be open-minded, to be open to every kind of experience. And I've tried to write my honest feelings as articulately as possible.

- **Did it occur to you when you were very young, that you'd be in a position of the most powerful critic in America?**

Frank Rich: When I was very young, my parents would buy *The New York Times,* particularly the Sunday paper, and I would be fascinated by it. The idea of the power was not what really interested me. I was vaguely aware of it. What interested me was the idea of writing for a publication which is read by a lot of people who love the theater. No other newspaper or magazine of general interest in the United States devotes so much space to the theater. That makes people care about the theater writing in the *Times.* The exciting thing about being here is writing for people who share your interest and have very strong opinions, and feelings about it. So, yes, I did fantasize about doing it.

The power thing historically has always been said about *The New York Times.* I'm working on a book about the history of the theater, and I've learned that whoever the *Times,* critic has been, there always has been this mythology. There's nothing that the critic in the job can do about it. I try just to forget about it when I'm writing, because if you start thinking about it you become paralyzed. You have to keep the reader in mind and all you can do is: be honest. If you start saying, "Well, the *Times* has all this power, I better not say what I really think, because I don't want to upset people, or the show might close," then you are engaged in self-censorship, which ultimately defeats you as a responsible critic.

- **You've said that the standards you stand up for are these of "good theater." What's your idea of "good theater?" What's your hierarchy of theater values?**

Frank Rich: To me good theater is theater that involves the mind, the senses, and the feelings. But there's no hierarchy. There's some great theater that involves primarily the intellect and maybe doesn't touch the heart, or vice versa. I find most exciting theater that's not just a literary experience, that has some reasons for existing on the stage, that cannot exist anywhere else. If a play could exist as a book or as a movie, it's flat for me. I don't generally love completely realistic theater, unless it has a poetical dimension, such as in Chekhov, whom I do love, or a different kind of dimension—much more modern—like Brecht. I've less sympathy for the more melodramatical, naturalistic kind of play, which could as easily be on *TV*. To me, even the good Shakespearean movies don't capture the quality of the play on stage. I'm also a partisan of theater that's a visual experience and has very little literary in it—the whole line of Mayerhold which goes against Stanislavsky. I like Peter Brook. But I'm open to all sorts of things—the theater is constantly changing and you have to be open to everything.

DAVID RICHARDS

There've been always three things that I have been interested in: French language, theater and newspapers. And all my life I've tried to combine them. Sometimes I'd be studying theater in France, and that would take care of the two of them, or I'd be writing about the theater in the United States, but that didn't have anything to do with French. I've always thought the best job for me would be theater critic of *The Herald Tribune* in Paris.

I was an actor for a while. I studied theater and I had the chance of joining the Hillberry Repertory Company, which is part of Wayne State University, in Michigan, and sort of a regional theater made up of graduate students. You earned a doctorate in theater and you paid for your studies by acting in the company. The same week I got accepted into that company as an actor, I got an offer to work for *The Washington Star*—then the afternoon newspaper in Washington, D.C. It was a clear choice: did I want to go into newspapers and write about theater, or did I want to be part of the theater and perform? And it seemed to me that writing about theater was not only something I did better; I also figured that there was more space in the newspapers to be filled than there were roles to be played.

So I became the theater critic of *The Washington Star* and I was there from about 1968 to 1981. In 1981 it was the first major metropolitan newspaper to close. As soon as they closed, *The Washington Post* hired me to be their theater critic and I stayed there till the middle of 1990. This whole period in Washington was time of theatrical explosion: there were at least 15 theater companies. The Kennedy Center got a lot of shows before they went to New York. So you generally saw the best of Broadway and also a considerable body of work created for Washington alone. I once estimated: I spent at Arena Stage the equivalent of a whole month round the clock. The regional theaters not only would do contemporary plays, but they would do classics, so you got a huge range of productions to write about.

And I've been at *The New York Times* since August 1990.

I come from New England. It's a puritanical place: emotions are not expressed overtly; you operate on a subtext; you don't always say what you feel; what is not spoken is much more important than what is said. That's a wonderful preparation for being a theater critic, because most plays are subtext. I would even say: a New England upbringing prepares you to understand subtext. I remember the first time

I saw a play—I was about seven or eight years old, and to be that close to the emotional life of other human beings and yet safe, because you were not implicated— well, I just wanted more and more. And I think, in the long run, the reason I ended up as a theater critic is simply because most of what I've found out about life, I've found out through plays. It's the form that speaks to me most directly. Some people can listen to a symphony and understand the cosmos. I can't. Some people have a film sensibility. The best way, the only way, for me to understand the world is this medium—a play: live people enacting life.

GORDON ROGOFF

My interest in theater goes back to my childhood. I was four when my mother first took me to a Broadway show—a musical. I remember that I was standing up— I was too small, and I was fascinated by the theater. Oddly enough, it began with that and also with Fred Astaire and Ginger Rogers' musicals and movies, and I thought I wanted to be a tap dancer. Later on I was directed by my father to be a high school English teacher. That's because he was such. But the kind of a secret life he had had earlier (which I learned about much later) was that he had wanted to be a playwright and he'd studied at Harvard in George Pierce Baker's 47 Workshop. Eventually, when Baker was forced out of Harvard, Yale took him over and he was the founder of The Yale School of Drama. So there's a kind of connection going on, because I ended up at The Yale School of Drama in 1966 with Robert Brustein and I'm there now also.

Having decided not to be a playwright for whatever reason, my father was determined that I would not become a theater person either. So I began with that typical father-and-son conflict, which I think is a very boring Arthur Miller play. The problem was simply that he didn't want me to suffer, he saw the theater as an insecure way of making a living. The consequence was that I was protective about my theatrical ambitions; I kept them from him. After graduating from college, I said I was going to spend the summer in England and study Shakespeare at the Shakespeare Institute, and he thoroughly approved of that. I did go but, unknown to him, I had also arranged to audition for the Central School of Speech and Drama in acting. Once I got there I did that, and I got into the school, and I wrote home and said, "I'm studying and you have to support me!" As it cost so much less in those days than anything I might have done in the United States in graduate school, there was very little he could do. So I stayed and I studied acting in London, and that changed my life.

It changed my life not because I became an actor—I did actually a lot of acting at that time, but that was not what I really wanted to do. I found out that acting was only one avenue towards understanding of the drama, better than studying the plays alone, especially if you were interested in directing, as I was later. Through all of that I became interested in all aspects of the theater, and what happened in the rest of my life is an improvisation: I didn't think about a career; I tried simply to jump at opportunities that seemed to be very interesting. In a naive way I've always assumed that if I wanted to do something, I could do it.

In England I founded a theater magazine, *Encore,* with one of my fellow-students and eventually we had another student on the board of editors, Vanessa Redgrave. We took it out of the school and rather rapidly it became much more than just a school magazine, and the result was that I was automatically an editor and a writer. When I came back home, at one point I found myself working in TV as a story editor.

Later I worked for the Actors Studio as the administrative director (I'm the only one who ever had that job). I was very anxious when I was asked to do it. I thought very passionately that the theater was a wonderful instrument for social involvement. I took the job and lasted in it for two years. It was extremely difficult. Among other things, the difficulty was Lee Strasberg. He worked psychologically on people in ways that I was trying to escape. I was not interested in being his son. I had had quite enough to handle with my own father. But I learned a lot from the work with actors. What I did for him, however, was: he wanted to initiate a new division of the Actors Studio in directing, and, to my surprise, he asked me to form the unit and he never interviewed any of the people I did. I didn't think I was really qualified to do that, but I did it anyway. At the time I had to go underground. I had to make my telephone unlisted, because many of the people in favour with Strasberg would give me calls in the middle of the night and threaten my life. So I left and I really never saw him again. I became momentarily an editor for a wonderful magazine, *Theater Arts Monthly,* which existed for 46 years. I was an editor there from the 45th year.

In 1966 Robert Brustein asked me to join him at Yale and I stayed with him until 1969. I had the same problem with him as I had with Strasberg: I couldn't always say, "Yes! Yes! Yes!"

After leaving Yale, I went to Chicago and Buffalo, and I spent the better part of the next six years mainly in Buffalo, teaching and developing my own theater company. I didn't write very much in those days. Before that I spent time as a critic in association with the Joseph Chaikin's Open Theater. I found out that Chaikin and the improvisational work with the actors was exactly the opposite of what was being done at the Actors Studio. In 1975 I had an offer to head the Theater Department at Brooklyn College and I took it as means to get back to New York. I missed New York and I also missed seeing the theater, and following it, which could only really be done in New York at that time.

In the '60s I began writing for *The Village Voice.* Then I came back and forth. At the end of 1979, I began writing there on a regular basis, which I did up until 1991. I don't want to do regular reviewing anymore.

So I've been moving always between the practical side of the theater and writing about the theater. And in the in-between I've been teaching. And that's the irony: my father wanted to make me a teacher and I ended up a teacher. The joke was on me. On the other hand, the joke was also on him, because I did what I wanted to do, meaning that I'm still involved with the theater; I was not sidetrack from it as a teacher.

JOEL SIEGEL

In Los Angeles, when I was a little boy, there was almost no theater at all. I didn't start going to the theater until I was in high school. My parents grew up during the Depression in the '30s, and my grandfather couldn't afford to give my father an education. My father was an electrician. Because my parents couldn't get an education, I always knew that I would get it and because theater was culture and something to aspire to I was impressed by it. I'm also interested in music and in art. In college I majored in history and I wanted to be a writer. That's what I've always wanted to do and I still think of myself basically as a writer—I write reviews.

When I graduated from college, I stayed in graduate school getting a Ph.D. in history for a little bit, but I didn't really want to be there and I ended up into the army. I went on my own terms, so I was able to avoid Vietnam and then I came back, and I got a job as an advertiser in an agency in L.A. I was also writing as a free-lance for magazines and newspapers, and I was working on a very underground radio station part-time—just for fun.

Once I got a phone call from someone at CBS News in New York. They had read something that I'd written in a magazine and they had realized that I was the same person from the radio station. So they called me to audition for TV. They were looking for someone to cover rock-and-roll music and the counterculture, and surprisingly they hired me. This was 1972, and I was the first person to regularly cover rock-and-roll music and to interview Steve Wonder, Bette Midler, Ray Charles on TV. I moved from CBS to ABC, because people in this business tend to move— when you move they pay more money and that's nice.

First, I was a feature reporter, doing anything five days a week. One day they were auditioning for a film critic and I went to the news director and said, "Why don't you give me a chance?" He said, "Go ahead!", and in a week I was on the air doing film. The job in New York is that when you do film you also do theater. It was 1876, so it's more than 15 years now.

- How did your Broadway "adventure"—writing the lyrics of the musical *The First*—affect you as a critic?

Joel Siegel: It helped and it hurt. Now it's very difficult for me to give a negative review to a play because I know how hard people work. When you give negative criticism to a movie, everyone who's made it has already been paid, the work is done. But a play is a living thing, and even the smallest play involves 30 or 40 people. There's a saying in Hollywood, "Nobody ever sets out to make a bad movie." I don't think that's true. People do set out to make bad movies and they don't care. But I don't think anyone ever sets out to give you a terrible night in the theater. People want you to enjoy what they are putting on stage.

- Do you think that it would be better if more of the critics have some kind of practical experience in the theater?

Joel Siegel: I don't think it makes any difference.

- But for you it has done so.

Joel Siegel: Yes, but you can push that argument to extremes, and it's very dangerous. For example: does that mean that I would be incapable of reviewing a play about

a woman because I'm not a woman, or a play about childbirth, because I haven't..?
You can't say that. But it's important for people who review theater to know as
much about the mechanics of the theater as possible. One thing that I've learned
from doing a musical is how difficult it is to change it once it's set. There're certain
critics who'll sit back and say, "Well, they should have done this and this, and
this." I never do that because I don't think that's fair.
- **Do you have any ideas for another musical?**
Joel Siegel: Oh, yes, more than one, but I don't have time yet.

JOHN SIMON

My father loved books and my mother liked to go to the theater, but not passionately.
He was Hungarian, she was Yugoslav from a Hungarian minority. I was born in
Subotica, Yugoslavia. Then we moved to Belgrade, so I consider myself a Belgradian.
When I was six, seven years old, our school participated in a production at the
National Theater in Belgrade, and I walked across the stage pretending that I was
an aristocratic gentleman. I had no lines, but walking across that big stage was
a thrill. I was even more interested in poetry though, and I liked movies. I went
to a good secondary school in Belgrade, and, for a year, to an English public school.

When World War II broke out, my father, who was a big businessman, and another
industrialist were in the United States, negotiating business deals. They asked their
families to join them on tourist visas. By the time we reached Havana, the Nazis
had overrun Yugoslavia, so we exchanged our tourist visas for immigrant ones.
First, I went to a school in Pennsylvania, later, in New York. Then up to Harvard,
where I majored in English, and eventually got a doctorate in comparative literature.
In between I was in the army.

In college and in the army, I occasionally did some acting. There was a well-
known drama school in Boston, and during World War II there were not many
men around, so the drama students were mostly girls. They put ads in the Harvard
paper for young men who wanted to act there, and I went and did some acting.

When I got my doctorate, paradoxically, I stopped teaching and went into
publishing. I worked for a book club, The Midcentury Book Society, where I was
the editor of the house magazine. What made the job worthwhile was that the Society's
editors were three very distinguished men: W. H. Auden, Jacques Barzun, and Lionel
Trilling. Meanwhile I was offered the job of the No. 3 art critic on *The New York
Times,* but I didn't get it because I couldn't agree with the Sunday editor, who wanted
me to do some purely journalistic pieces. So I became a free-lance, writing articles
on literature, film, and the arts, until the job of drama critic at the *Hudson Review*
opened up and I got it.

That's how I became a drama critic. But that magazine is a quarterly and it doesn't
pay very much, so I wrote also for many other places—for *Theater Arts,* for example,
where Gordon Rogoff was an editor and Eric Bentley published frequently. I then
did drama reviews for Public Television for a while, but I was too tough (that has
always been a problem!), and there were protests. I delivered a negative review
of Marlene Dietrich' one-woman show, and her fans organized an attack on me,

and I was fired. (Years later, Dietrich herself wrote me a nice fan letter.) For a year I was the drama critic for *Commonweal,* a Catholic magazine, a fine publication, but with little money and a small readership. It's like writing inside a black hole. I wrote for various other publications, however, which made me a little more visible.

In 1968 *New York* magazine asked me to become their drama critic. Whereupon some people started a movement to have my predecessor, Harold Clurman, reinstated and me fired, but not much came of that. So, ever since, I've been at *New York.* I started out as a drama critic but after a few years a moment came when they switched me to film criticism. Two years later, it was felt I was too tough on movies and it was safer to have me in the theater slot, so I was moved back to that. While doing theater at *New York,* I was also film critic for *Esquire* for two years in the early '70s. That was the only time in my life when I had equally important jobs in film and theater. Otherwise, it's always been a better job in theater or a better job in film.

- People say that whereas Frank Rich is the most powerful critic in New York, you are the most hated one. What do you think of that statement?

John Simon: That means that I must be doing something right. Anyone who has read enough must know that out of what has been written over the centuries maybe half of one per cent survives (which means 99 1/2 per cent must be bad); therefore, to say much more often than not that something is bad means simply to speak with the voice of history. Obviously, though, it has to come from an inner conviction. You can't just say: because 99 1/2 per cent have been proved bad by history I'll now say 99 and 1/2 times bad things, and then I'll say something good. You also have to have liked the rare right things. But when you look back over the years and it turns out that you've said nine times as much bad as good, that in itself is perfectly normal and natural.

However, this is known to make you more enemies than certain other critics have, who don't have that proportion of unfavorable reviews to favorable ones, and therefore to be hated in this field is quite different from being hated as a doctor or bus driver. I'm not saying it's pleasant, but it is unavoidable, and one has to live with it. I've often said, because I happen to be a gregarious person, I'd like to go to more parties than I do, but I get invited to very few precisely because I am "the critic John Simon." So I have to live with that deprivation.

- What hasn't stopped amazing you in the attitude of the others towards you?

John Simon: When somebody writes in a letter protesting my review of a certain play, that I don't like anything, even though this play was reviewed along with two or three others, one of which I thought was magnificent. And what I also find amusing is that people come up to me often in the street and say, "I'm probably the only person who really likes your criticism. I always have to defend you." Another thing that happens fairly often, which I find rather nice, is that young people who write criticism in some other city come and say, "I'm known as the John Simon of Chicago" or "I'm called the John Simon of Houston!"

- One of the main accusations against you is that you attack the physical appearance of the actors. What do you think about that?

John Simon: We need beauty in the theater. An actress who is genuinely talented but not beautiful should definitely do what she's doing. However, if she were also beautiful, it would be a plus. And I would print such a statement, as almost no other critic would. If I've accomplished anything, it is that some of the younger critics have begun discussing and criticizing looks. Physical beauty is a wonderful thing and it should be looked for and rewarded. Of course it's even more wonderful if the actress makes you forget that she's not beautiful, if a plain woman can make you believe that she's beautiful with her acting. I'll kiss her feet for such an accomplishment. But it doesn't happen very often. On the other hand, if an unbeautiful actress plays the part of a comic, unromantic, or specifically unattractive person, looks don't matter; but if she plays a heroine with whom we are supposed to fall in love, it helps if she's beautiful. In real life you can fall in love gradually, for all kinds of nonsurface reasons, but in the theater you only have a few minutes to do so, and beauty is the best short-cut, always excepting a very great talent. And then one keeps hearing, "You are a critic, you know about good theater, but your opinion on who's beautiful and who isn't doesn't matter!" I don't see the difference. I don't see why one shouldn't be praised for being beautiful if one can be praised for being intelligent. Intelligence is just as much of an unearned miracle as beauty.

- Do you happen to regret any of your critical judgements?

John Simon: Oh sure! For example, today, there was a tribute to Mary Martin, and my wife, who adores Mary Martin, reminded me of something I had written about her, of which she says I should destroy every existing copy. I agreed that I shouldn't have written that. There are other things I regret from time to time—the way everyone makes mistakes. Every waiter sometimes spills the soup on a customer, or on himself. But if you make too much of that, it can paralyze you for the rest of your life. I've also overpraised people sometimes.

- For example?

John Simon: Oh, it's hard to remember everything you've written. The only people who could answer your question precisely are the ones who are so narcissistic, who take themselves so seriously, that they can quote themselves endlessly. As a rule I don't remember things like the wittiest thing I've ever said, the best or worst reviews I've ever written. To remember such things means paying too much attention to yourself.

ALISA SOLOMON

I was working in the theater when I was a high school student and I was, in fact, one of the people, who founded the Steppenwolf Theater in Chicago. I went to school with some other kids who started that theater and I was its stage manager for its first three years. We were 17, 18, 19 years old. In college I studied drama as well as philosophy, and then I was at The Yale School of Drama in the Criticism and Dramaturgy program.

I came to New York hoping to work as a critic and a dramaturg. When I f first came here, I wrote to *The Village Voice* and I sent them copies of some academic articles I'd written, but they totally ignored me—I didn't even get a courteous reply.

Then, about nine months later, they wrote to me and said that they needed somebody at that point, so could I send them my clips again, and so I did. That was about eight years ago. Together with writing for them, I'm teaching full-time at one of the CUNY colleges—English and journalism. Sometimes I also teach a reviewing course in the journalism department.

EDWIN WILSON

No one in my family was involved in the theater, but both my parents enjoyed it and they started taking me to the theater when I was quite young. I grew up in the South, in Tennessee, but I came to New York periodically with my parents and I invariably saw a lot of theater here. My father was a businessman and he probably wanted me to be a lawyer or a businessman. I majored in English at college and I took a year of graduate work in English. After that I went to work in the coffee business for three years, and then I decided I really did want to get involved in theater. I applied to the Yale School of Drama and I went there. I've been involved in theater ever since.

At Yale I was the first person to get the D.F.A. degree—just by accident, I happened to be there when the program was started. I stayed at Yale a year after I finished my course-work and taught one class in playwriting while I wrote my dissertation. Then I taught for two years at Hofstra University on Long Island. Then I came to New York and was involved in some directing and some Off-Broadway producing during the early '60s. About 1967 I was offered a job at Hunter College, teaching playwriting, which I began doing. About a year and a half later, I was offered a full-time job, teaching playwriting and history, and theory of criticism at Hunter College. I moved to the Graduate Center at City University of New York about 1988/89.

In 1972 I got a job as the theater critic for *The Wall Street Journal,* which I've been doing ever since. All my studies at Yale and my teaching gave me a good background for being a theater critic.

LINDA WINER

I was raised in Chicago in a middle class family. My parents had little interest in the arts. I studied music my whole life and my degree is in classical music. I never had any early interest in journalism at all. I thought I was going to just get a doctorate in musicology and go on in music. Also, I'd always been interested in dance.

In 1968 I won a Rockefeller Foundation Fellowship for the training of classical music critics. It was administered by the University of Southern California. It was a wonderful program which only existed for about eight years. It was the first and probably the last time that any foundation invested in training critics and they only did it in music, which is unfortunate, because they should have been able to do it for dance, theater or something else. There's always been an assumption in this country that you can go to school to learn how to build furniture, but for criticism, you are supposed to just somehow be hatched. It really is a very haphazard attitude for something that, unfortunately, has as much power as it does.

This was a two-year program, very intense. They picked only four people from the country that year. They brought critics from all over the country and some from London, and the four of us would go to concerts and write reviews, and these critics would critique our reviews. The second year was an apprenticeship and I was an apprentice at *The Chicago Tribune,* where I stayed for 11 years. I was an assistant music critic for a while. I was 22 years old, and at that age, it was wonderful for me. So I didn't have that struggle that most people have breaking into a newspaper. I sort of fell in because of this. I was very lucky.

When I started, in the early '70s, it was right at the beginning of the dance boom in this country, and there was a lot of interest in dancing. I was in the first dance critics training program in the summer of 1970. I'm a product of all these different programs. I became more and more interested in dance and started writing about dance. I went also to the theater a lot. The person who was the theater critic of the paper was basically interested in Broadway road shows. This was a bad time for those, whereas it was a very good time for the Chicago regional movement, which was just beginning and which wasn't covered much by our paper. I volunteered to do it, because I felt we should be covering it. The first new play I ever reviewed was David Mamet's first play *Duck Variations.* I watched Steppenwolf Theater grow up from a little theater in the basement in the suburbs. I watched the first productions of Gregory Mosher, and I wrote about them. So I eventually stopped doing music and became the theater and dance critic.

I moved to New York in 1980, because the *Daily News* had tried to start an afternoon paper—one that would possibly be more upscale—and they hired a bunch of people. I went there for a while, but it was so insecure and I wasn't doing criticism per se. The experiment folded in ten months, but I got saved. The people who began *USA Today* called me and said they were beginning a new newspaper and they asked me if I wanted to try, and I thought, "Well, there's nothing to lose, as long as I can keep on living in New York, it'll be interesting." So I was at *USA Today* for five and a half years as sort of a critic at large: I covered all the Broadway, Off-Broadway, and most of the major regional theaters that were considered to be of national interest. It was a wonderful experience, except that I had to write in these little tiny slots. After a while the limitations of the form got to me.

At that time *Newsday* was expanding into New York City. They already had a theater critic, but they came to me and asked if there was anything they could seduce me over here with. I had read the paper a lot and I liked it, and they had really wonderful columnists, but nobody wrote a column about the arts. So I proposed an arts column, which they liked, and I moved to *Newsday,* where I've been since 1987. I wrote the column twice a week for the first year and a half, and then they made me the chief theater critic, which means that I do a general culture column a week and a Sunday theater column. I also do the major reviewing.

2   THE GRAND MASTERS:
THE CRITICS AND THEIR
MENTORS

Robert Brustein

Dennis Cunningham

Michael Feingold

Mel Gussow

Holly Hill

Jonathan Kalb

Walter Kerr

Frank Rich

Linda Winer

They answer the question:

- **Who do you consider your mentor in theater criticism?**

ROBERT BRUSTEIN

I was more influenced by Eric Bentley than by anyone else. He was the first one who made us all see that the theater could be a place of seriousness, dealing not only with serious ideas, but with serious metaphysics and emotions. And we are all still fighting that battle of trying to persuade Americans that the theater is a serious place, not just fun and games.

DENNIS CUNNINGHAM

Walter Kerr was my hero. He is my mentor although he doesn't know it. Actually I was taught by somebody that he taught. So in a way... That was a hell of a theater critic. I miss his writing, that mixture of know-how and savvy, and sheer intelligence, but represented in this very lovely way. Nobody has that touch.

MICHAEL FEINGOLD

The main influence on me, the main example, is Bernard Shaw. But among my teachers, I have five fathers, spiritually speaking: Robert Brustein, Eric Bentley, Richard Gilman, Stanley Kauffmann and Gordon Rogoff. They're all in their different ways engaged in practical theater work and one of the things they've taught me is that

31

you must know how theater is really made. The greatest defect of journalistic criticism is that people simply do not know what it is they're seeing and how it's made. Consequently, they have no way to analyze the effect that it's had on them; all they can do is respond to the effect, "I like this," or "I don't like that," or "This is very powerful!", but they don't know what the source of the power is.

MEL GUSSOW

Harold Clurman. He was not only one of America's most important directors, producers, and teachers, he was our most astute theater critic. Because he was a working man of the theater, he could go to a play and differentiate between performance and direction, which is one of the most difficult tasks we face. I envied the fact that he reviewed from a historical perspective. It was an education to be with him.

HOLLY HILL

Harold Clurman, who was my teacher at Hunter College. He had such a love and tremendous enthusiasm for the theater. To me he's the ideal critic, because he came out of the theater himself.

This is another reason he and Walter Kerr were such good critics—they were practicing theater people, who worked on both sides of the stage. Harold Clurman also knew music and art, and politics in a way that he was a kind of Renaissance man. Then, Ed Wilson of *The Wall Street Journal*—one of my teachers and dissertation advisers. Prof. Glenn Loney—also one of my dissertation advisors. I was very lucky that I had encouragement from a lot of people who were wonderful critics.

JONATHAN KALB

Stanley Kauffmann. In my writing it has meant a great deal to me to know that there exists out there someone who reads on his level and who also cares deeply about theater. It's very easy and tempting to lower your standards when writing about the theater because the impression you get is always of writing into a black abyss. Theater critics don't get mail. They do sometimes, but it's usually hate mail. The typical letter is, "You bastard, if it weren't for you I could've gotten that grant!" You never get letters of gratitude, or letters arguing with you intellectually. I've been writing professionally for 12 years, and in all that time Stanley is the only person other than the editor I was writing for or the person I was writing about who has ever said "thank you." "Thank you for bringing those ideas and those bits of prose into the world. I feel richer for having read that." That generosity of spirit along with his intellectual honesty have meant everything to me.

WALTER KERR

I don't like to say, "This was the only one." But certainly George Jean Nathan would be one of them.

FRANK RICH

Walter Kerr: when I was a child I read him in *The New York Herald Tribune.* Then, Kenneth Tynan, when he was working for *The New Yorker.* Tynan and Kerr have the biggest influence on me. Walter Kerr, later as a dear friend of mine, influenced me greatly as a critic here—at the *Times.* He's certainly the major influence on me in terms of style of writing and the way he conducted himself in job.

LINDA WINER

A woman who doesn't get enough attention anymore, who is very dear to my heart: Claudia Cassidy. Because she was such a power in Chicago, it didn't seem all that strange for us to have other women critics in Chicago. It wasn't until I moved to New York, that I realized how strange that was. There aren't very many women theater critics in New York, that's for sure.

3   LIFE RELIVED: A FANTASY

Robert Brustein
Dennis Cunningham
Mel Gussow
William A. Henry III
Stanley Kauffmann
Howard Kissel
Stewart Klein

Edith Oliver
Frank Rich
David Richards
Joel Siegel
John Simon
Edwin Wilson
Linda Winer

They answer the question:

- **If you could turn the clock back, would you do it all over again?**

ROBERT BRUSTEIN

I'm still doing it, so I must be relatively satisfied. I'm restless and obviously like to move around in various guises. I do sometimes yearn for a life in which all I have to do is just write, reflect, and read, but I'm not ready to enjoy that life until I retire. So until then I'm happy to jump around like this.

DENNIS CUNNINGHAM

I would certainly choose to have that experience. Yes. But I'm ready to do something else now. I remember interviewing Beverly Sills, when she took over as an opera administrator. I asked her: won't she miss singing? She said, "No," and she had a little pin that said IDTA, and I asked her, "What does that mean?" She told me, "I did that already!" meaning you should do it but then go on and do something else. I actually have a strong urge right now to go back to teaching, but this is not an immediate plan. And acting, too. I'm talking about two or three years from now. But who knows? I've certainly been very happy with this TV experience, but I do miss being on the other side of it too.

MEL GUSSOW

Yes, but if that clock were in a time-machine, I might transport myself back in theatrical history—to England in the '50s when Beckett and Osborne were introduced;

to Broadway in the '30s during the heyday of O'Neill and the American musical; to the late 19th century when Chekhov and Ibsen were revolutionizing drama.

WILLIAM A. HENRY III

Yes, but I wouldn't want to be exclusively a critic. I like the actual situation I have in which I do other things—both in *Time* and elsewhere—at different lengths, on different subjects and even in wholly different media, like TV and books. I've always worked along the borderline between arts and politics. I'm interested in the ways in which our politics mirrors our culture and vice versa, and the pieces I like best are pieces that do both. I have a hard time imagining a life in which I was not responding to the culture of my time. I'm a better critic for the fact that I spend a good deal of my time thinking and writing about other issues, everything from AIDS to Olympic basketball, because it means that I'm much more ready to see how a work of art relates to the rest of society and not only to itself or other work of art. I find most boring criticism that teaches in terms of strictly an aesthetic continuity, as though the arts were entirely a thing apart—criticism that is concerned mostly with displaying the scholarship and erudition of the critic, rather than inviting the audience into the tent.

STANLEY KAUFFMANN

I'd be a musician. That's what I'd like to have been most of my life. Although I know that the profession has its hardships and stupidity like every other. But would I become a critic again? No. If I could choose what I wanted to do and there were no obstacles, I would choose to work in the theater in some way—not as an actor— but as a director. But that's a mere fantasy. Looking backward I certainly have no regrets about having been a critic, because it's by my standards a worthwhile thing to have done. You've made some small contribution. Every once in a while I get a letter from someone, who makes me think so. I don't think that as far as my criticism is concerned, I've wasted my time. Other things, perhaps, but not the criticism or the teaching.

HOWARD KISSEL

By and large I've enjoyed reviewing theater. Had I pursued my original choice, acting, I think I would have been even more frustrated. Instead of playing character parts in Shakespeare and Moliere, which was my ambition, I would have played idiot roles on TV sitcoms or, if I had been lucky, in movies. In these meaningless arts I would have added to the meaninglessness. It would not have been a satisfying career.

Criticism has given me a way to participate in the theater in what I hope has been a meaningful, intelligent fashion. Because I love the theater so much it means a lot to be part of what is left of "the theater community."

STEWART KLEIN

I don't think I would have become a theater critic. I might have still become a journalist, but I might have specialized in some other form of it.
- **Don't you wish to see your reviews written?**
Stewart Klein: No. But I do have a dream. Everybody in TV gets fired sooner or later, and it eventually will happen to me. My dream is that I then sit down and write one little book that becomes a best-seller and then it's turned into a play, and the play is turned into a musical, and then it's turned into a movie.

EDITH OLIVER

I never chose it. It chose me.
- **Would you like to be chosen again?**
Edith Oliver: Oh, I've enjoyed the job. I love all these free tickets.

FRANK RICH

Definitely—yes!

DAVID RICHARDS

A career in criticism was inevitable. Whatever it was I discovered in the theater, the theater was going to be a major part of my life. I can see that now. Maybe I might have persisted as an actor. Maybe not. But I can't imagine a life without theater in it. The only other thing: I wish I had started playing tennis, when I was six. I started playing tennis five years ago. If I could start all over again, I might just choose to be a professional tennis player.

JOEL SIEGEL

Oh, yes. I have the best job in the world. They pay me a lot of money to do things that other people pay money to do. It's just wonderful! It's not just the entertainment and the enjoyment of it, but it's also being able to learn. I've seen every Broadway play that's opened in the last 15 years—its fascinating! I'm really very lucky!

JOHN SIMON

Yes, because I think that you don't choose your profession, your profession chooses you, and there's no way you can escape that. I didn't become a critic immediately. I was a teacher for a while; I worked in publishing for a bit, but clearly those weren't the right places for me. There are psychological reasons for becoming whatever you are.

EDWIN WILSON

I would, because I've had an interesting mix of things in my life. I've been able to combine a number of activities that I really like, and that suit my personality, my temperament, my interests, and I've been fortunate, because very few people are able to do this. I've been also very fortunate to be my own boss most of the time: to set up my own hours as a teacher and a freelance critic and to move from one activity to another.

LINDA WINER

Yes, though this really was a fluke. It was nothing I had ever thought that I would do and, in fact, it has turned out to be as interesting a life as I could imagine having. It turned out that I love newspapers, which I didn't know before. They are very much like the theater—they create a new product every day, and that's very addictive. I like the energy.

All my life I had wanted to be a veterinarian. I love animals more than almost anything and I like science. Whenever I get bored, I think I'm going to become an animal behaviorist. There's always been this other tug in my life that basically that's what I was supposed to do: to love and help animals. I wanted just to live with animals and get paid for it and study them. And might still.

Part II
Know–How Of Criticism

1 A LOOK AT THE BASICS: PRINCIPAL PARAMETERS OF THE CRITICS' PROFESSION

Clive Barnes
Robert Brustein
Dennis Cunningham
Michael Feingold
Mel Gussow
Jonathan Kalb
Walter Kerr
Howard Kissel
Stewart Klein

Jack Kroll
Pia Lindstrom
Glenn Loney
Edith Oliver
David Richards
Joel Siegel
John Simon
Alisa Solomon

They answer the questions:

- **What's your idea/notion/definition of theater criticism?**

- **What are the main tasks of theater criticism?**

CLIVE BARNES

It is an attempt to act as a bridge between the audience and the artist, to try to make easier the way for the understanding of the artist. The critic is functioning at the highest level when he is interpreting and introducing the art to the reader. The critics' opinion is subjective but it has to be an informed subjectivity. He ought to know more than the readers he's writing for; about the art, the scene, the pragmatic side of the theater, what constitutes the plays, the history of the drama, and the history of anything else. Good critic is one with a special information and experience who can open up ideas for his readers.

ROBERT BRUSTEIN

Theater criticism should be both instructive and corrective. It should try to correct taste in the sense that it should point out plays that are overrated or underrated,

41

and it should also be an effort to understand the artist and the artist's work, to analyze it, and explain it.

DENNIS CUNNINGHAM

If it's for an academic publication, it's very high toned; it assumes that the reader has an intense interest in the theater and a knowledge of it. That sort of thing you can't do on TV. On TV you have to keep adjusting. You don't adjust your aesthetics and judgments, but you adjust how you present it—you don't make critical, classical allusions; your intention is to communicate. You might put it in a slightly less involved way. You can still be profound, as you know, the great classics are very simple.

MICHAEL FEINGOLD

There are four key things. The first one was formulated back in the early '50s by a critic who's not much remembered now, Robert Warshow. In one of his essays, he says, "A man watches a movie, and a critic must concede that he is that man." So the first thing is that you are a member of the audience, you see a play and it has an effect on you. If you're not guided by that in writing about it, then you dislocate. I know critics who, the minute the curtain goes up, open a notebook and bury their noses in it, making notes about the set, or the opening moment, and they don't see the rest of the play. There's at least one major member of the right-wing critical fraternity who, I'm prepared to say, has never seen an entire play.
- **Who is this person?**
Michael Feingold: I won't tell you! So the first thing is to feel the effect of the play on you. The second thing is to look at the play as objectively as one can and see what it is: what happens in it, what it says, what it represents. The third thing is to try and see what the first two things meant to the artist, what would be the purpose of doing this and having this effect on you. And the last thing is to try and see what larger meaning it has for the world. If one does those four things, one is a critic.

MEL GUSSOW

Harold Hobson said that James Agate, his predecessor as the drama critic of the Sunday *Times* of London, hoped to be remembered as a critic who never let anything second-rate get past him. Hobson's response was that he "would rather be a critic who never failed to recognize anything that was first-rate, however bizarre it may have appeared." While many critics might subscribe to the Agate principle, I would put myself firmly on the Hobson side of the fence. Certainly it is important to identify the inferior, but it is necessary to identify works of quality and of promise. Through history, masterpieces have been misjudged and misrepresented in their time. It was Hobson, for example, who understood and appreciated the value of *Waiting for Godot*. This does not mean that a critic should simply be an appreciator. Necessarily he is judgmental; negativism comes with the territory. The critic's first responsibility is to himself—and to the art he is criticizing. One should be true to what he thinks of a work and uninfluenced by anything extraneous, such as the reputations of the creative participants. One has to try to understand what the playwright is trying to do and then to measure the validity of that aim. A critic should be able to describe and analyze a play vividly, to characterize the performance so that a reader feels he is receiving a firsthand impression. Critics should be provocative.

JONATHAN KALB

To follow an idea up to the end—that's my notion of a good piece of criticism. I believe that you can't be a good critic if you are not frustrated with your job. There's a real failure of ambition in most newspaper writing about the theater; it's written by people who are satisfied with who they are and what they are given. I think you have to demand more. As soon as you have a little formula for how to write, say, a 500-word review, you're dead. I still have to pull out my hair on each assignment, trying to solve the problem of how to write a short piece that is both interesting to read and that says something worthwhile about the artistic effort in question.

If you have no practical experience in the theater you have nothing but your paternalistic judgement to offer. You haven't got the counterbalance of sympathy for what it takes to put together a production. You might think you do but you really don't. You have to have been there and gotten your hands dirty.

WALTER KERR

The job of the theater critic is to tell the readers how the last night's show was. You owe it to your reader, who is giving up his time and who is coming to you for serious advice. You hope that you'll succeed in persuading them that this is good or bad, or worth paying money for or not.

HOWARD KISSEL

The job of the critic is to determine: What were the intentions of the playwright and the actors? Did they fulfil those intentions? Was it worth the effort? These are the tasks of the daily reviewer who writes for the casual reader, someone who is not necessarily interested in the art of theater but occasionally likes to go and wants a general understanding of what is happening.

There is another criticism, directed toward a more serious reader, who wants to know how the play in question figures in the context of contemporary theater. The most interesting criticism is one that explores the relationship of the contemporary theater to the world around it. That is a kind of exploration I get to do very seldom.

Someone once said that criticism arises out of a depth of love. Though criticism is obviously a rational activity, there is something irrational and even quixotic about the depth of our passion for this mercurial and often exasperating art. Love for the theater should be discernible in everything a critic writes.

STEWART KLEIN

I don't have an exact formula. I do go back to the basic rules—a critic should explain three things: what is the author trying to say?; has he said it?; was it worth saying? If you answer those three questions, by and large you've done your job.

The critic is not only a bridge between the author and the audience. He's also a kind of consumer advocate, especially in New York, where theater tickets now cost $60. And let's face it: many of us, whether we like to admit it or not, are entertainers. A lot of people like to read or listen to criticism, even though they never have any intention whatsoever of going to the theater. They want to hear what you have to say about it. It's news, and reviews are expected to be entertaining as well as informative. In that respect, we are performers.

JACK KROLL

When you go to the theater and see a play, it's an experience like any other human experience. In this case you are experiencing art, and the first thing you've got to do as a critic is to write something about the nature of that experience. For example, when you go to see a play by Chekhov in the end of the 20th century, what's happening to you? Somehow you have to give this feeling to another person who's reading your article. That's the most basic thing, the most fun, and the biggest challenge. If you pick up the works of George Bernard Shaw from 1890s and look not just at pieces …… about Ibsen or Shakespeare, but about plays you've never heard of—they are vivid and important to you a 100 years later, because he evokes life; he makes you see and hear the actors and actresses; he tunes you into the experience. The opinions have faded away, but the human reality is what counts. When you read what Stark Young …… about *The Glass Menagerie*, the amazing thing is that he immediately understood all about Tennessee Williams from his very first play. This is another thing: to make discoveries! Then, the critic has to give a sense of the performance. Not only, "She's very good; she's not so good!", but: What's the special thing that comes from the stage? These are the things the critic has to do first and then to make some ultimate judgements.

Also, you want to teach your readers. Not in the academic sense of the word. But you want to give them a kind of revelation. In the old days, I used to get a lot of letters from teachers saying, "I used your piece on so and so in my class." That used to give me a lot of satisfaction. I remember I did a story about *The Beggar's Opera* and I got a letter from a professor, who said, "Your piece put everything in context better than I did, so I use it in my class now."

Another thing: you are writing for a mass audience and you have to have it in mind. You want to take them and sort of lift them up. That's what gets editors scared. They say, "Our audience don't care what you say about *Hamlet* or Pirandello!" That's not true! You have to make them care; you have to make them see that this is part of their life. The critic should try to point out how art affects readers' lives to an extent they are not even aware of. Maybe they've never read *Ulysses*, nevertheless, it has affected their life. Maybe they've never looked at Picasso, but he has changed their life, whether they know it or not. And you have to point out that in such a way that an academic audience would be able to read it, too.

I've had lots of arguments with friends about the mixed writing [including excerpts of interviews in the reviews]. They say, "You violate the purity of criticism." And I say, "Well, maybe we shouldn't use the word criticism then. I consider myself a cultural journalist." Most of the drama critics around the country are, in fact, reviewers, which is entirely different thing. Criticism happens when all the elements I've mentioned begin to get into it. And criticism can be very stimulating. If a critic is really brilliant and if you disagree with him, it starts a whole process of thinking.

PIA LINDSTROM

I look at my job in a practical way. No. 1 is to hold the viewers. I'm not speaking to people who necessarily go to the theater. I may be on the air and what they really want to know is what the weather will be or who won the baseball game. Maybe they hate theater. The review has to be a good review, regardless of what the play or the movie is. I look at what I do as my own tiny product. I want to present it in a way that will capture the attention of the audiences. I try to be funny; I try to be humorous whenever I can. The other part is to let people know what's going on even if they are not going to go see it. I'm telling people what I saw, what it looked like, who was in it, what I thought of it.

GLENN LONEY

A critic is somebody who should have a background in practical theater, who should have a great deal of knowledge of theater history and dramatic literature, and who takes an overview. To go to see a play and merely to write about it is not criticism; it's reviewing. Criticism would be: a week, a month, a year later looking at a production with an overview on a higher level, comparing it with other productions of something similar or other productions of the same play, and dealing with ideas, rather than, "She was very pretty.", and "He forgot his lines.", and "I liked this scene."

What a good critic does is to interpret, to elucidate. It's not just to kick people in the teeth. Especially with a very new work, a critic can be so helpful or so destructive by the way in which he or she reaches the reader. You didn't see this show, for example, but you might see it after reading the review. Or you saw it and said, "Oh God, what a mess!", then you read a thoughtful review and said, "I want to go back and see it once more." Good criticism is when another critic will say, "God, she is a good writer! I didn't like that before, but after reading her review, I like better what I saw!" The best kind of criticism not only helps the audience, but it also helps the artists. You say, "It's such a wonderful idea, and they had such energy on the stage, but in the third scene they might try doing so and so," and the smart director may say, "Oh God, he's right!" And it should be fascinating, provocative to read as well!

EDITH OLIVER

It's reviewing; it's journalism. It's your obligation to tell your readers honestly what you've seen last night. If you do it right, sometimes you don't even have to put in an opinion. There isn't a reviewer in the world, and certainly not in New York, who doesn't want to like what he sees. The force of bad reviewing is the force of disappointment. We all want to love it. There is no point in being a critic, if you are not stage struck.

DAVID RICHARDS

First and the foremost, criticism is descriptive. It has to say: what is this thing called a play? What does it look like? What does it smell like? Is it skinny? Is it fat? I believe that plays are like human beings and they should be talked about like human beings. They are not these dry, abstract, intellectual objects. A play breathes; sometimes it gets excited, its blood races fast; sometimes it goes to sleep. Plays have a biological life. To talk about them in terms of the intellectual content— that's part of it, but such a discussion tends to put off people. Meanings are something you come to afterwards. Afterwards you can say, "Oh, yes, this play is about ambition and hard times." But you don't go to see ambition and hard times. You go to the theater for some kind of an emotional experience. You go for the ups and downs, the twists and turns. It's important that criticism acknowledges that. You get people interested that way. It says: Here's this living, breathing object. Let's go see how this object behaves. People like to observe behavior.

So, you have to identify the object. Then you recount some of the feelings, the ideas, that you experienced while living through the play—somehow passing that on the reader in a language, that's vivid and exciting and might possibly compel him to undertake a similar trip.

Criticism itself should be interesting. You should want to read it just for the pleasure of reading it, not because it's necessarily going to lead to some action or lack of action on your part. It should have some intrinsic life of its own. I do believe it's a legitimate literary form.

JOEL SIEGEL

Criticism implies a distance, something deeper and more important than what I do on TV. When I review a film or a play, I like to think that every once in a while I might say something that's valid for the people who are involved in the creation of the art work and that they could benefit from it. But my audience is the TV audience; it's not the artists. In real, serious criticism, the audience is the artists.

JOHN SIMON

The critic essentially has three roles, and none of them is more important than the other. He has to be a teacher, because he has to continue the education of the people who read him, who have stopped being students; we have all stopped being students too early in life. He also has to be a creative writer who writes as well as a poet or a novelist or a playwright, so as to make reading his criticism a pleasure rather than a duty. And third, he has to be a thinker: he has to think about the world in the context of the play or book he's reviewing. If you do all these things, you've really done your job. Of course, the trouble is that usually you don't have enough space to do all this, so you have to stint a little: the good critic almost always has more to say than he has space for. The final courtesy to the reader is to figure out which of the things you'd like to say are less important, and to concentrate on those that in the particular case are more so. Also, a theater critic has to be tough, open-minded, and sophisticated: a cosmopolitan person, who knows about many other things besides his field.

ALISA SOLOMON

The main principle for me is to always write about what it means that a particular play is being done in a certain way, in this place, at this time. I think of it as cultural criticism, and therefore it's political—the questions of: why is anyone doing that play?; what does that mean for us?; why is it being done in this way?; and, of course, all the other sorts of things: how well is it being done? and so on, but those are secondary questions to me.

2 ENTER PUSHKIN: CRITICS FACE A THEORETICAL CHALLENGE

Criticism is science for discovering virtues and shortcomings of the works of art and literature. It is based, first, on perfect knowledge of the rules which guide the author in creating his work; second, on profound mastering of the paragons of art; and, third, on active observation of the phenomena of contemporary life .

Alexander S. Pushkin

Robert Brustein
Dennis Cunningham
Michael Feingold
Jeremy Gerard
Mel Gussow
William A. Henry III
Holly Hill
Stanley Kauffmann
Stewart Klein

Jack Kroll
Pia Lindstrom
Frank Rich
David Richards
Gordon Rogoff
John Simon
Alisa Solomon
Edwin Wilson
Linda Winer

They answer the questions:

- **What do you think about Pushkin's idea of criticism in principle? To what extent does it overlap with your notion of theater criticism in particular?**

- **What are your main objections to Pushkin's definition? What would you add to it?**

ROBERT BRUSTEIN

It's a fairly accurate description of criticism. Pushkin is quite right that the critic is trying to represent or recognize the rules by which an artist writes. The fact is that a critic quite often imposes his own rules on the artist and on the arts. The major conflict that goes on through history is between something like the Academy Francaise, that has a set of rules—the unity of action, of time, of place—and says you have to conform to them, and a playwright, like Corneille, who listens to this idiocy and says, "Oh, I've got this play about a big war with a hero named the Cid, and how can I compress a war into one day, and have it all take place in 24 hours?" So he says, "Well, I'll just pretend to conform to those rules, but meanwhile I have to follow my own demands and needs." That is the basic struggle between the critic and the artist: the critic wants form, logic, functionality, rules, and the artist is just blasting away, trying to find some avenues for freedom.

DENNIS CUNNINGHAM

That sounds right to me. Especially the first one, because it is the one that a lot of people don't have. You have to know how it works in order to be able to judge it.

MICHAEL FEINGOLD

All of that is perfectly true, except I found it startling that Pushkin, who after all was a poet and an adventurer in the Romantic sense, should be so concerned with science and rules. If I were rewording that definition, I would take away those two words and say that criticism is an art, and that there are no rules; that artists may create according to a form, but they don't create according to rules. The things artists do that seem wrong are usually the most interesting and brilliant things they do. When Bernard Shaw, who's my real model as a critic, talks about the rules of harmony in music as described in what was then a standard textbook of harmonic structure, he says, "I'm sure all these excellent followers of the rules may be very nice gentlemen in their own way, but I prefer the music of Bach, Handel and Mozart, and none of them ever bothered for one minute about whether they were following the rules or not." The critic should be objective in the sense that you look at the thing as clearly as you can, but unscientific in the sense that you always know it is you looking at it and not anyone else. That's where you have to take pains not to make the audience think that you are the only pair of eyes in the room. I've seen critics fall out of their chairs laughing at a scene in a play, I mean literally, and I've seen the same critics go back to their offices and write that the play was badly formed, and not mention to their readers that they fell out of their chairs laughing. And I've seen them carp at the acting of some novice and not mention that the audience gave this totally unknown person a standing ovation.

JEREMY GERARD

It's a wonderful definition. I agree with it wholeheartedly. I did't hear anything in it about love for the art. I would add that the love for the art makes the critic excited to be going on even when 90 per cent of what he sees is mediocre.

MEL GUSSOW

The statement has value, but criticism is less a science or even an art than a craft. Were we to have the time and space of literary critics, it would be more of an art, but as practiced today it is necessarily a journalistic profession, one in which we try to express ourselves as artistically as possible.

WILLIAM A. HENRY III

What Pushkin suggests is very much the kind of criticism that I try to do. Where I differ with him is that I don't think it is science at all. Yes, one tries to have the knowledge of what guides the artist, some of which knowledge comes from looking at the work. In terms of understanding the paradigms of art, one thing that makes them an uncertain guide is that they change with the times.

The best critic is acutely aware of the political and psychological trends of his time, and is able to look at art in the way that the anthropologist would, as a cultural artifact. The best justification for writing about art is that it illuminates larger questions of human existence. The reason that we as a people take interest in culture is that in the long run it is what defines us. Political systems come and go. Economic systems come and go. Look at Poland! It has been dominated by Lithuania, by Germany, by Russia; it has rarely been run by its own people. But what defined Poland through all that was its culture. Culture is what is enduring and indigenous, and it ultimately expresses itself through works of art more than anything else. To justify the study of the arts in the popular press, not for the limited audience of artist-practitioners but for the mass audience, one must rely on the idea that the arts are a mirror of what is going on at the moment politically and a mirror in the long term of who we are as a people and as a human race. Therefore, to be aware of contemporary life phenomena and their historical antecedent is the best preparation for being a critic. That enables you to answer the most basic journalistic question, the one that hits hardest in cultural coverage; that is, "Why are you telling me this?" Every story needs to answer that question. Why does the reader need to know? And the reader needs to know because somehow what is being told illuminates larger questions of his existence. He doesn't simply need to make a decision about spending time and money going to see something.

This higher intellectual rationale especially holds true for publications like mine, in which the majority of the readers, being geographically scattered, are not making their consumer decisions at the moment they are reading about theater pieces. They are reading because they want to know about the larger world. It's an approach that would help a critic in any kind of publication because it makes him more of a journalist, a first-draft writer of history, and therefore much closer to the higher purposes of the overall journalistic enterprise.

HOLLY HILL

Pushkin's rules can be applied to any kind of criticism. He's left out one thing. My teacher, Harold Clurman, emphasized that it's tremendously important not simply to know as much as possible about contemporary life (meaning culture, politics, sociology), but also to be as cultured as possible about the history of music, painting, philosophy. In other words, ideally the critic knows everything. But, of course, no critic knows everything. There are many critics, for example, who know very little technically about music. I'm one of them and I've been taking music courses for years trying to make up for my lack of knowledge. And there are other critics who don't really know the history of dramatic literature; they may be familiar with some of the great works in the canon, such as *Hamlet* and the *Oresteia*, but they haven't read all of the Greek tragedies; they haven't read or even seen Shakespeare's minor works; they may not even know who Kleist is, and they may only know *Mary Stuart* of Schiller. I'd say the majority of the critics, talking about the whole country, not just New York, are not familiar with anything more than the major canon. So Pushkin's is an ideal definition. I don't know who were the critics Pushkin was thinking about, but we have to consider that, in most countries that I'm familiar with, critics are required to be journalists or broadcasters and they are generally taken from the ranks of people in journalism or in broadcasting, not necessarily and not usually people educated specifically to be critics.

STANLEY KAUFFMANN

There is a fourth thing. Jealousy. Every good critic wishes he could be a good artist. There is not a critic alive (and there are some great ones, whom I admire: Eric Bentley, for example) who wouldn't rather have been a great artist. But my own choice was that I would rather be a good critic, I hope, than a second–rate artist. Looking back, sometimes with very mixed feelings at the things I've written, I think that I write best about the plays, or books, or films that I wish most I could have done. In the theater, let's leave out names like Shakespeare, I don't wish I could write like him; who could wish that? But Beckett, Pinter, the best of Sam Shepard—I write about them fairly well. In films, I think about people like Antonioni, Bergman, Kurosawa. If I had that talent, those are the kinds of films I'd like to make. There's much connection between good criticism and what you might call admiring jealousy or jealous admiration.

I think, if I might be so bold as to criticize Pushkin, that criticism is not a science. It's an art which involves the three points that he's made and needs also humility and pride. Oscar Wilde says that the critic's work is more difficult than the artist's, or more refined, because the artist works with life, and the critic works with what has been made from life by the artist; therefore criticism operates on a higher plain. Wilde is being slightly witty and cynical. But there's some truth in it.

STEWART KLEIN

I'd agree with that absolutely a 100 per cent. Of course, not many critics meet Pushkin's qualifications, but one tries the best one can. A few people would arque about criticism being a "science." Somebody once said: a critic is like an eunuch in a harem. He watches people making love every night, he knows how love should be made, he observes how love should be done the best way possible, but he can't do it himself.

JACK KROLL

There's always been controversy about precisely that point: is criticism a science? I think, what Pushkin has written, in this respect, comes out of that particular period when he has lived: it's part of the Enlightenment in general.

When you bring the first two points to the art it gets a little tricky, because who says what the rules are, and who says this is the best? If you look at the art of the modern world, it's certainly doubtful that you can discover rules which are applicable to what artists everywhere do. In this sense it's amazing how much the whole idea of what art is has changed since the last century. Pushkin would be astonished at the state of affairs in criticism today. Now his very careful definition seems so simplistic. Criticism has become more complicated: you have to know a great many things that maybe you didn't have to know before. T. S. Eliot has said, "The only method is intelligence." He meant, I think, that if you don't have a certain kind of intelligence, it doesn't matter how many rules and how many things you know, you are going to be a lousy critic. Also, there's a greatly out-of-fashion word: taste. Clement Greenberg talked a lot about taste. I don't think you can be a good critic if you don't have taste. Taste detects authenticity; it detects certain qualifiers which, if they are not there and your taste says "No," then this work of art may be very interesting, but it's not successful, because these mysterious intangible values are not there and the relationships of the energies are not balanced. When Eliot says "intelligence" and Greenberg, "taste," I think they are really saying the same thing. Or maybe you combine the two of them and then you have a critic.

The third point of Pushkin is exactly right. You can't be a critic if you just specialize in what went before. Goethe has said something very much like that: it's absolutely crucial to be a contemporary person.

PIA LINDSTROM

In general all these things, I'm sure, are true. Who would I be to argue with Pushkin? But that's much too elevated for American TV. I have a fairly wide range of knowledge on lots of things, and I've seen a lot of things, and I like the theater; I bring a certain enthusiasm to what I do, and they can depend on me. But the only part that has to do with what I do is the third one: putting in context what the movie or the show says to us today. For instance, if it is treating women badly, that's something that someone like me would notice.

FRANK RICH

It's a good definition. I would particularly emphasize the third point, because you can know everything about the art and the theater, but if you don't know anything about the world then you exist in a vacuum. To me the worst kind of criticism is a lot of academic criticism. You have to compare things from the theater not only to things from the theater. Life also has to enter. You have to understand life, because it's part of the equation—who you are.

One point I would add is: you can understand life, but you also have to be able to write. If you can't express what you want to say in a way that grabs people's attention, all the knowledge is useless. Furthermore, in addition to understanding the rules of art, you have to be a reporter. Whatever your ultimate judgement will be, you have to be able to describe what happens on the stage as a witness for the people who didn't witness it. As a reader of criticism, I feel that the more successful is that criticism which so vividly makes the event come alive that leaves the readers room for their own judgement. If a critic puts all his cards on the table and describes what he saw, and doesn't just give an opinion, but explains by what experiences and analyses he's reached that opinion, a reader can say: I see why this critic didn't like it, but the event is so clear to me that I know my taste is different from his, and half of the reason he didn't like it is a reason I would like to see it. To me the test of the good critic is his ability to make someone go and see something that he didn't like. That's for me the ideal. That's why I've enjoyed critics like Kenneth Tynan and Walter Kerr.

I try to go to the theater with an open mind. When I sit to write I try to figure out how and why what I've seen did what it did to me—whether I was bored, or excited, or amused, or stimulated. You've got to be ready for plays that break the "rules" of art, too. Criticism is an art, not a science.

DAVID RICHARDS

I'd have to think about that. It's interesting: I have all these university degrees, but I don't think about criticism in academic terms. I think about it as a journalist does. Pushkin is writing academically, so we could debate it, but it doesn't seem to apply to me.

GORDON ROGOFF

Sounds good. The only part I disagree with is the perfect mastering of the rules. I don't believe in rules. I do believe in Good and Bad. I suppose that those who believe in Good have to be masters of the Old and the New Testament. Our Old Testament is Shakespeare and that's actually one of the bitter jokes: many people involved in the theater, including some who would be critics, don't know Shakespeare. I could be very specific. Our very talented students in the dramaturgy program at Yale in a sense confessed to me—I made a poll of what Shakespearean plays they didn't know—that there are few of them who've read all of the plays. Yet they're eventually going to be dramaturgs and critics. I find that quite distressing.

JOHN SIMON

Pushkin had the benefit of living in a rather more orderly age: an age that was less hellbent on crazy experimentation, on defying every known rule, on indulging the most outlandish aspects of anybody's ego. So, in a more structured society with a more structured theater, what he says is perfectly fine. But today, to speak of perfect knowledge of the rules when there no longer are any? How can you know them perfectly—or even imperfectly? Or to speak of "mastering the paragons of art"—who knows any more what the paragons of art are? And if anyone thinks he knows them, he uses them only to kick them over. Now it's much more a matter of intuition, of what is called gustatory criticism; you put it in your mouth and you taste it—if the taste is good, it's good; if the taste is bad, it's bad. But you have to use your own intuition, knowledge, and preferences, which may be fair or unfair, because nobody is free of some prejudices. The point is, however, that there's no such thing as objective criticism; but one should know that, as a human being, one is subjective, and try not to indulge the subjectivity any more than is absolutely necessary. One should be subjective objectively. Impartiality, if it were possible, would be the prerogative of God—in whom I don't believe— and not of a human being. And it is not even necessary, because criticism is an art, and not a science, and you cannot give an artist a formula for writing poetry, plays, or novels. *He* is the artist, and *he* has to do what he thinks best. Then it's up to other people to evaluate it. In a similar way, the critic is creating his criticism, not merely evaluating something. The evaluation is up to the rest of the world and to the future.

ALISA SOLOMON

That definition is a good place to depart from. It's one of those traditional ideas that everybody should digest, so they can then get rid of it. I don't know if I would call criticism a science, first of all. The prose style is very important to me and I don't know if I'd go so far as to say that it's art, but it's not scientific writing. Secondly, I don't think there's anything objective about criticism. Then I don't think any playwright writes by rules, and the plays which most conform to rules are the ones that are the least interesting. So maybe I would challenge the wording of that all and say that it is important to know the intentions of the playwright. Obviously you can't criticize performance art according to the standards of naturalistic dramaturgy. I'd use the first principle that way. The second is absolutely necessary, certainly. The third one we talked about when we spoke about criticism in principle.

EDWIN WILSON

How can you argue with that? It sounds excellent. As it concerns the "science part," I think that he's presumably speaking somewhat metaphorically.

LINDA WINER

I don't think criticism is a science. It's an extremely subjective thing. When people think about an objective review, it's a contradiction in terms. A review is already your opinion, and your opinion is already very subjective.

When I was starting in Chicago, there were four thriving newspapers. Getting up in the morning and reading four reviews of the same event, it sounded to me as if these people had gone to completely different events. It was a good education for me in terms of realizing that the arts are complicated, that human beings are complicated, and that reactions are complicated, and that's part of what makes it so interesting. If we were to divide it up into little check-points—check off your first three big criteria, the rules and so on—it really dehumanizes the arts, takes away the juice that makes them. I don't think we hand out the answers. It's much richer a process than separating into parts, which isn't to say that we aren't analytic. But if you go to the theater with this little yardstick, and you come to measure and you already think you know what you are going to measure, you may be measuring something that is really not that important. You have to let it happen to you first. You have to stay open as much as you can.

3 CASTING TIME: THE ROLE OF CRITICISM IN THE THEATER PROCESS—IDEAL AND REALITY

Clive Barnes
Dennis Cunningham
Michael Feingold
Mel Gussow
William A. Henry III
Holly Hill
Jonathan Kalb
Stanley Kauffmann
Howard Kissel

Glenn Loney
Frank Rich
David Richards
Gordon Rogoff
Joel Siegel
John Simon
Alisa Solomon
Edwin Wilson
Linda Winer

They answer the questions:

- **What do you think is the ideal role for theater criticism to play in the overall theater process?**
- **How can it be compared to the situation that exists today in this field?**

CLIVE BARNES

Once Sol Hurok—one of the last of the great impresarios—told me, "You know, what's the job of critics? It's to sell tickets." And I said, "Your idea might be right. But if critics have to decide which tickets they want to sell..." Without question, criticism is the most valuable publicity the theater can get. But the critic is writing for the audience, for his readers, rather than for the artist. People talk about the importance of maintaining standards, but I don't think the critic does that. If the critic were to maintain standards, he would set up those standards; he would write plays. And I cannot write even a bad play. I can see when it is bad. But I'm not a disappointed playwright. Obviously criticism is not meant for the artist. It's a private conversation between the reader and the critic. On the other hand, if two people have a conversation about you, you are going to eavesdrop. You'll say, "Oh, my God, they are saying that I'm an idiot, that I'm beautiful, that I'm doing this or that." And you'll take it personally. It's a difficult situation.

57

One of the difficulties we have is that most of the things we call criticism are not criticism at all. We tend to say: someone is a critic, and someone is a reviewer. In America, particularly, they call reviewers the critics they don't like. In fact, we are all reviewers—people who write about an event—whether it is an art exhibition or a play, or a movie. Criticism is about the art itself. When Aristotle wrote the *Poetics*—that's criticism, but when you go to the New York Shakespeare Festival and write about a play—that's reviewing. It doesn't matter who does it or where it's done. Criticism of the art is almost an art itself, and it can have meaning to the artist. All the artists can learn from reviewing is what an intelligent member of the audience is saying about them. It may be useful. He or she will learn about the reaction, but not that much about the craft.

DENNIS CUNNINGHAM

Ideally, theater criticism should guide the audience and, by the same token, guide the creative people.

MICHAEL FEINGOLD

I don't believe theater criticism has any role in the process of making theater. I don't think it should. It should exist primarily as an art in itself, and the process of making theater should be dealt with by the theater artists and the audience, and there should be no interference. On the other hand, when you write criticism that is an art in itself, what you do is influence people in the same way a work of art influences people: it has far-reaching consequences of a kind you can't envision.
- **So you absolutely separate theater criticism from what it criticizes?**
Michael Feingold: No, I wouldn't separate them. What I would say is that they are both part of something much bigger. It's not like a man at the counter of a store saying, "I'll buy this, I want that for a dollar!", and another man coming over and saying, "Oh, don't buy that, buy this, because I know better than you!" I don't believe that criticism should be a part of that experience. There should be a simple transaction between the artist who says, "I have this for sale!", and the audience which says, "I want this.", or, "I'll try it and if I like it I'll buy it again!" There should be no critical interference with that process. If on the other hand, you say to someone, "Oh, they have an interesting sale there!", and then the person goes there and finds he likes it, that's something quite different.
- **But it's also a kind of interference.**
Michael Feingold: No, it's just a passing remark. It's from outside. It never hurts to send the people to the store where they can make up their own mind whether to buy it or not. The interference is when you come to them in the store and say, "I tell you not to buy that!" That's totalitarianism.
- **But do you think that if the critic is in the store, to continue with your metaphor, people will take what they've been told by him/her for granted, without thinking?**
Michael Feingold: Yes, that's the tragedy of American culture. There's no help

for it. The daily papers have been in the store so long, people mistake their opinions for the truth. I'm a pessimist. I don't think Americans like being informed, or making up their own minds. They like being told what to think. Especially the rich, oddly enough.

MEL GUSSOW

Often theater professionals regard us with suspicion or hostility. To them, our primary purpose is to write rave reviews, which they can excerpt for use in advertisements or on theater marquees. Anything less is considered a dereliction of duty. Criticism does not play much of a role in the theater process. Many artists swear they never read reviews; others consider us the enemy, and in interviews they tend to disparage or at least to dismiss the critics even when they have been instrumental in their careers. Occasionally it is suggested that critics be invited to witness the rehearsal process. That can only lead to a distortion of perspective. Ideally a critic is a wise and judicious counselor rather than a judge and jury.

WILLIAM A. HENRY III

The role of theater criticism is opening the audience's eyes to works of art, helping to raise the level of debate. I think that artists are served badly by critics because critics ought to be able to understand more, to be both more perceptive and more willing to take risks in interpreting a work. Most artists say that they never get anything out of a review, that there's no possibility for dialogue. But in principle, there's no reason why criticism cannot contribute to a higher understanding of arts. There have been, in the past, some critical writings that helped move literature forward. Usually those critics were not only smart, but were engaged in some way in the arts. They were in some sense participants in the struggle.

HOLLY HILL

Theater critics should serve both the audience and the theater community. A critic serves the audience by being an informed and insightful commentator on the event, so that the readers can get a sense of the event, and if they wish to follow that critic's influence and make their decision about whether or not they want to spend their money--which, given Broadway and even Off-Broadway prices, is not a small decision. Critics serve the wider readership by making a historical record about what's going on in the theater. They serve the theater community by drawing attention to the growth of artists.

The critic also has to serve himself or herself. You have to think about your own standards, because if you think first about your readers or the theater community, you are likely in some cases to pull back from your own best judgement; to say, "I don't think it's her best work, but I know that she's been having a hard time and I don't want to hurt her." The more the critic loves the theater, the more the serving one's own standards comes into play.

JONATHAN KALB

I'm sure you've gotten the same answer from every critic you've talked to. Ideally criticism is a dialogue with artists, but there seems to be a taboo against the theater artists coming to words in response to criticism. There's silence on the other side, so it ends up being just a monologue. That's not the spirit I'd prefer to work in. I'd love nothing more than to have someone—a director, a playwright—publish a response to my commentary on his or her work. Then I could publish a response to that or not, and so on. But it just never happens. Most of our theater journals don't even have letter columns anymore, and that's a shame. It just reinforces the idea that we critics are nothing but curmudgeons who say "Thumbs up!" or "Thumbs down!", "Four stars" or "Three stars." Of course, the typical theater artist will say, "But my language is the theater." That's not quite fair. People in the theater talk among themselves incessantly and articulately. They talk as audience members at each other's shows, and spectatorship is part of the theater process. Talk about theater happens *mostly* among people who are not theater critics, and I know from personal knowledge that a lot of them can write perfectly respectable letters. It's no defence to say prose-writing isn't your medium.

STANLEY KAUFFMANN

The best critics want something for the theater beyond their jobs. They don't think that, if they see a play and write a readable review about it to tell the people whether to see it or not, that's enough. The play has to be put in some context of what I want the theater to be. That's why Shaw is great. Every time he writes a review about a stupid musical, he writes an analysis of what that musical was and where it stood in relation to: a) what a musical should be, and b) what the theater should be doing. Most critics who write today don't have any idea about that. The trouble with them is that they have no other ambition than to do their job well. The best thing about Brustein, with whom I have great differences of opinion, is that he wants something for the theater and he hopes his criticism is a way of moving the theater towards it. I don't say that you have to have a theater of your own like Robert Brustein—he's the only one who does—but the best of the critics like Alisa Solomon, Jonathan Kalb, Michael Feingold, have some idea of what they would like the theater to be. It's not at all a question of saying: this play must be judged against the perfect ideal of a theater. Of course, that would be stupid for most of the things they write about. But by and large, criticism should be growing out of a philosophy of the theater.

HOWARD KISSEL

Right now I think it's very important for theater criticism to remind people that what they've seen is not very good. Critics also must remind the artists that they are part of a tradition that these days they are not upholding very well.

There's an old tale about a kingdom where the harvest has been bad. If people eat bread from this grain they will go mad. Fortunately in the king's storehouse there is enough grain for one person to eat until the next harvest and remain sane. There is a meeting of the king's counsellors to decide who will be the one person to remain sane. Of course, they all insist the king should eat the good grain. But he, being an unusually wise king, says, "That would be very dangerous, because there would be no one to check my power. If there were no one to check me, heaven knows what I might do. I'm going to appoint the wisest of my counsellors to be the one person to eat the good grain. His job will be simply to remind all of the rest of us that we are mad."

In the current climate of New York theater, that's the role of the theater critic: to be the one sane person to remind everyone, "This is not good work!" That's not a happy position, but until the next harvest, that's our job.

- **Do you think that your colleagues realize that?**

Howard Kissel: Perhaps I take a darker view than some of them. Sometimes I have the feeling that some of them are enjoying the recent harvest.

GLENN LONEY

A really good critic could say, "This scene is touching, but it could be more touching if the lights are so and so, or the director should restage." But it should be done by people who understand theater. Walter Kerr was one of the few critics who had worked in the theater. He would give a little advice, and Harold Prince might have a rehearsal on the next day to make some improvements, or the playwright might make some changes in the play to clarify. Harold Clurman also. It is certainly the job of the critic to be useful to the theater community by being perceptive and knowledgeable. Therefore, I don't agree with the idea that *anybody* could be hired as a critic, and that seems to happen a lot of the time. But here I'm talking only of production aspect. If the director seems to have missed the point of the play, that certainly also should be discussed. But then the critic may have missed the directors's point, too.

FRANK RICH

I don't really know what the role of criticism is within the theater itself. My role is to stand up for the people who go to the theater.

Frankly, the playwright doesn't need to be told by me or by anyone else what to write. Writers write what they believe in. Many of the brilliant things in the American theater have been written unexpectedly. The best people in the theater, or in any art, occasionally learn something from a critic, I'm sure, but basically the thing has to be in their hearts and their minds. If they have to write by guessing what a critic or an audience, or a government will like, they are dead. I don't feel the critic's place is to be sort of a cultural tzar who says, "This kind of playwriting is bad, and this is good!" I've never tried to do that.

The critic has to identify with the audience; he has to be the audience' eyes and ears. If the critic starts to identify with the theater to the extent that any "serious" play he sees should be given an encouraging review, even if he thought the play was boring or fatuous, or a play done by prominent theater people should receive an extra credit—if extraneous factors like that tamper with the opinion of the critic—the critic's judgement becomes worthless. Those extraneous considerations about the theater wreck the equation between the critic and the reader that has been built up through trust over a period of time.

- You've said that the mass audience has much lower taste than the critics. And on the other hand, you've said that the critic has to identify with the audience. Aren't you in contradiction with yourself?

Frank Rich: What's successful in the mass market place of culture is generally of a lower taste, whether in TV, cinema, theater, books. But generally speaking, the New York audiences are extremely sophisticated and that makes it all the more important that I be honest and keep the high standards that I believe in. When I get mail complainings from readers, it's much more often when they feel I've been too kind, I've been too indulgent. Only people in the theater think I'm too hard. But in New York, where so much is competing for the peoples' time and money, people don't want to be patronised by a critic and told that they should see something that's a waste of their time and money. They're tough and they know what they like, and you cannot impose your taste on people who are intelligent and have always been. That's the reason why New York has been and even now is the center of American theater. The audience here is smart.

DAVID RICHARDS

A critic over time can help to elevate taste. I know in Washington, for example, I was very helpful to Arena Stage. I probably helped the audience along. It would be interesting to ask Zelda Fichandler because I was there for 20 years and what I said as a critic particularly affected that theater.

The eternal problem is how to help assure the survival of theater. And you don't do that by being indiscriminately encouraging. In the long term, you hope to make people care for the institution of theater itself even if specific examples along the way are not good. That's what I'd hope to do: foster an enthusiasm for theater in general. Theater criticism is a hyphen, that is: it translates sometimes complex and difficult works to a broad audience of readers.

GORDON ROGOFF

A comic way of addressing that is to say that, in the theater process, the critic is the obstacle to be overcome.

- And in a serious way?

Gordon Rogoff: In a serious way, the critic is somebody who might be read long after the event, so that people who've done the work might find out what it is they've done. The best criticism is descriptive. The critic describes what he or she has seen, and that might be of some use to the artists. But in most cases, even if it is a very strongly positive review, the moment to read it is not the moment that you've just emerged from the new work. I remember Peggy Ashcroft, many years ago, saying that she never reads the reviews, even though she hears the news whether they are good or not so good. That if they are very good, she has no right to read them, because she shouldn't agree, and if they are negative, she would obviously not want to agree with them. Also, I would say that I don't for a minute imagine that the artist is that much interested in hearing from me.

- **When you were a director, weren't you interested in what critics said?**
Gordon Rogoff: I would generally not read them, at least not right away. I took my cues from Peggy Ashcroft.
- **Whom do you have mainly in mind when writing criticism?**
Gordon Rogoff: Mainly the artists.
- **So you are writing for them and you don't expect them to read your criticisms?**
Gordon Rogoff: I wouldn't suggest they read it until a year later, when they can look at it without too much involvement.

JOEL SIEGEL

The critics come after the process, and there are responsibilities to two separate groups of people, and the responsibilities are at odds.

I'm responsible to the audience and, unlike the newspaper critic, people know my face, so I go out and I say, "You have to go see this even though it costs $200. That's going to be the greatest night in your life!", and I run into someone on the street who says, "I spent that $200 and it stank," and people are going to punch me in the nose. So I have to be careful because that's part of my audience. The other part of my audience I'm responsible to is the theatrical community, because I really love the theater and I think it is important to help nurture the artists, to try to encourage the audience to support something that may not be perfect, but might just be very good, and very good is O.K.

JOHN SIMON

It's important, though hard, and in some cases even impossible, for the critic to convince the rest of the theatrical world that he is not an outsider, that the critic is a part of the theater—a functional, helpful, necessary part—and that it's his wish to make the theater better, not worse. He may be too cruel in some cases, but it is a cruelty based on passion. It is a very foolish assumption a lot of people make about tough critics, that the reason they are tough (or what they call nasty, or even vicious) is that they don't care. It never occurs to these people, that you do all of these things precisely because you *do* care, and because you feel that the theater is a very badly behaved child, or dog, that you have to teach how to behave, not necessarily as an ultimate absolute, but as you can best imagine it. And you make your small contribution to understanding, and somebody else makes his small contribution, and together all these critics do create a mosaic of beauty, intelligence, and usefulness, which the theater needs. And if they are harsh, it should be understood that they are just as harsh on themselves: that they have probably thrown away things they've written because they thought them bad, that they have spent hours speculating about how to make a sentence say exactly what they wanted to. In other words, the same kind of stringency, the same kind of sternness or demandingness, applies to what you yourself do as to what you are criticizing. And if you can convince people of that, you'll have half the battle won.

ALISA SOLOMON

The most hyperbolic, the biggest claim: theater criticism should make the world better, and it does that not by making the theater better, necessarily, but by contributing to critical discourse. It's sort of a Brechtian idea: if people practice critical thinking about the world, when they go to the theater, talk about the theater, think about the theater, that enables them to think critically about the world itself. Criticism in some utopian world should contribute to that. It's part of a lively discourse of the emotion and intellect that takes place publicly. That's what it ought to do best.

Does it do that in America in 1991? Of course not . It's functioning as a consumer guide. First of all, very few Americans go to the theater, and most of our theaters are not that interesting to go to—of course there are exciting exceptions—and it is very expensive, so people want to know if it's worth their money. Theater has never been taken seriously in the United States really. It's pretty much considered some kind of an escapist entertainment, and that's often what's delivered. Literally, people don't write about theater; plays don't get published; intellectuals don't talk about theater. I don't think it should be an esoteric field at all. It should be popular, but it doesn't have a kind of status that allows for a serious discussion. So criticism then is undervalued.

- So critics are not to be blamed for that?

Alisa Solomon: Of course, not. There are some bad critics, but I wouldn't even blame them. There's a commercial reality. I would say: globally, capitalism is to be blamed! The theater exists here within a completely commercial structure. Also, the role of theater is changing as the culture becomes more and more TV oriented. Even if you read criticism of somebody like Eric Bentley or Stark Young, or even Kenneth Tynan, it's a different thing than what the daily reviewers are offering us now. Theater is not taken seriously; we get less and less space, so even on a paper like *The Village Voice,* where the editors have some commitment to the theater, what can you do in 750 words? For the writers who are beginning now, there's no place to go. I feel that even for myself; I don't want to spend my whole life at *The Village Voice.* I'd like to write in other publications as well. I don't know a single other place to write seriously about the theater and get paid for it. I wouldn't want Frank Rich's job at *The New York Times,* because I wouldn't be able to write seriously what I really believe in that newspaper.

- You've said that critics are not to be blamed for not playing their role properly. Yet, there should be some fault of theirs, too. What is it?

Alisa Solomon: To generalize: critics who are blameworthy are those who think of their job as being a consumer guide and don't think of it as anything more;

who limit themselves to a very narrow range of theater-going; who aren't open to anything below 42nd Street; who are lazy in their thinking and writing, and who don't experience other arts. It's the theater critic's job to go to the theater a lot, but also to go to art museums and concerts, and dance and all the rest of it. I don't think very many do.

EDWIN WILSON

Criticism should be something that gives the perspective of the event to all the people who are involved in a theater production and to the audience. It should help point out certain things, discourage bad practices, and encourage new talent. It's clearly a little bit on the fringe of the things, but as far as the whole mix of the audience and all that is concerned, it can play an important role.

In the ideal society, in which you have well-informed audience members, they'll be able to make up their own minds and they might read critics to get some sort of appraisal or ideas of what they have seen, but they won't depend on that.

LINDA WINER

The best we can do is set up conversation in the minds of the readers. I really have no intention, no desire to mold playwrights in my image. I don't write for playwrights, for actors, for directors, I don't presume to tell them how to do their jobs. Yes, if by reading something that I wrote they can learn something that is helpful to them—that's terrific, but that isn't in my thought at all. My job and my intention is to have a conversation with the readers, and obviously not just the ones who were there last night because no one could have employed me for writing for a thousand people.

A good critic is not a person who's right or wrong, but a person with interesting opinions. The least interesting thing about the job for me is telling people whether or not to go out and spend 50 bucks. I hate the consumer guide function. I hope when people finish reading it, they'll have some idea whether or not that sounds like something they might want to spend 50 bucks for, but I don't tell them: kill for a ticket or don't! Basically critics exist because people like to read them and they like to bounce their thoughts off yours, and that's why it's so wonderful when there are lots of opinions. It has become so much less interesting with fewer opinions.

4   TAKING THE BULL BY
THE HORNS:
AMERICAN THEATER CRITICISM—
CHANGES OVER THE YEARS,
PROBLEMS TODAY

Clive Barnes
Robert Brustein
Dennis Cunningham
Michael Feingold
Jeremy Gerard
William A. Henry III
Holly Hill
Jonathan Kalb
Stanley Kauffmann
Walter Kerr

Howard Kissel
Stewart Klein
Jack Kroll
Glenn Loney
David Richards
Gordon Rogoff
John Simon
Edwin Wilson
Linda Winer

They answer the questions:

- **What are the main problems American theater criticism faces today?**
- **Have the problems changed a lot during the years you've been involved with theater?**

CLIVE BARNES

There is one great problem and it's different from 20 years ago: there is such a shortage of responsible opinions. Nowadays, there is still a first-night list of critics (although nobody goes to the first night)—16-17 critics. But there are very few opportunities for writing serous criticism, and they are shrinking, too. When I came to live here, there were still seven daily newspapers, now they are down to three or four and that makes a big difference. Also, TV criticism is much more geared to the medium; it has to be cute, funny. So the main problem is the lack

67

of outlets for serous criticism, and as people read less, even the significance of what is being written is being reduced.

ROBERT BRUSTEIN

We've not attracted, except in a few cases, people of real intelligence and passion to this profession. When I went to Yale, I tried to train theater critics for precisely that reason: I thought we needed people with the background to know what they were talking about. I thought we could help reform things. And a few of our people are in prominent positions as critics now, like Michael Feingold of *The Village Voice*. But most of them couldn't find jobs. They were too bright for the magazines or the newspapers. The critics usually come through a hierarchy of the publication, from the sports page, or the dance page. They don't necessarily come from literature.

Another problem with American critics, and I'm not the only one to say that, is that you don't know what their politics are, what their sexuality is, what their position is in regard to the world. All you get is a kind of free-floating opinionating: this one hated that, or preferred this play to that. And it is based on nothing. As a result it doesn't have the same endorsement you sense when you understand what the principles of the critic are. A critic like Bernard Shaw, or Eric Bentley, when they were wrong about the merits of a play, at least you used to know what they believed in. But you don't know what most of us believe in.

DENNIS CUNNINGHAM

I often get the idea that some critics are just showing off in their reviews, "Am I not the clever one?" And there are other critics who really are writing for the employer, rather than for anybody else. Like, "I remember the 1930-something production." And they weren't even born then. There's a lot of that, "Let me impress the bosses!" kind of stuff. There's also an insensitivity to how it works, to what the creative process is. They say either, "Oh, it's the same old thing" or, "Why don't they give us the same old thing we love?" One thing that annoys me about criticism is that they won't let especially established people try something new. Like Neil Simon. They'll say, "It isn't as funny as it used to be!" when he's trying to do something totally different and not trying to be funny. There's a real rigidity. There's a lack of imagination, as to where the author's going.

MICHAEL FEINGOLD

The state of criticism in New York now is very, very low—less so in other cities— because the people involved in it are mostly people who wanted to become famous through a journalistic career, which means automatically that they are egocentric and petty-minded. (Fortunately, there are major exceptions to this.) They're also people who basically have no feeling one way or another about theater and its importance; they don't know what it means to go to the theater; they only like the idea of being able to tell people when to go and when not to go.

There's a constant movement towards the idea that each show is an object in itself; that it has nothing to do with the artistic development of the people who've made it, and towards the notion that "everything I like is good and everything I don't like is terrible." The way of categorizing things as either all good or all bad is probably the worst part of it. A lot of this proceeds from the fact that in New York, even though we have a great many partially subsidized theaters, we have never committed ourselves to the idea of a National Theater that is fully subsidized, so that the artists would be free to make their artistic choices. The theater in New York is always evaluated in terms of hits and flops, and the audience is assumed to want to go to hits because the critics say so. When you have this hit-flop mentality, it means that you categorize things according to whether they are familiar to you, or whether there's something new in them, in which case they are alien and peculiar, and should be thrown out. To these people, everything that's new is a horror and an interference. To me, everything that's new is very exciting. One shouldn't say, "This is terrible!", when one only means, "I don't understand this!" It tends to reduce the critic to a joke.

It's very interesting that boundary lines now are drawn more sharply than they used to be. The general group of reviewers in New York used to be very middle-of-the-road about everything. They gave young artists more leeway. Now, the more conservative ones feel challenged, and suddenly, in the last few years, everything has become very political. There's a large movement afoot to drive out of the theater anything that doesn't fit the old schema. Fortunately, there's also a new group of critics, and some of them are rather well-trained and conversant in theater, and some are people of a solid general intelligence who keep calm about things, so they can go out of a show and say, "I don't like this, but it's very interesting!" Linda Winer of *Newsday* is one of these people. Her view of theater is basically middle-brow, but I don't find that offensive; she's reasonable about it. When she says, "I don't like this!", she implies that other people may very well do so. She leaves the audience to make up its own mind. But some of these people speak as if they were God and it was their power to decide that anything they don't like must be driven out of the temple with a whip; they think they're Jesus.

JEREMY GERARD

The main problem is that, with the exception of very few newspapers, it's not a very highly regarded job. It has traditionally been a dumping ground where editors put people who are either over the hill or not very useful in other places, and it's not seen as the specialized area that it is. The exceptions are places with active theater industries, like New York, Los Angeles, San Francisco, Chicago. The biggest problem in New York is that there are too few educated voices, and, as newspapers disappear, there are fewer and fewer. Several years ago, I attended a revival of a play from the '40s—*The Time of Your Life*. I found it very curious and I decided to go see what the critics originally thought of it. I went to the Lincoln Center Library and there were 13 overnight reviews, ranging from *The New York Times* to the Yiddish newspapers. The *Times* has always been the most important voice but still there has been a concert. Also, theater critics are expensive for newspapers because they write for very specialized audiences.

WILLIAM A. HENRY III

The main problem is the disappearance of the top-level, especially in the commercial theater. In absolute terms, the number of Broadway productions is down—between 30 and 40 the last few years, and in most years it's been closer to 30 than 40. So let's say there are 30 productions during perhaps 45 working weeks for you in the year. That means that you've got a Broadway show in only two weeks out of three—and that's at a rate of one a week. Hardly a full-time job! There's an immense amount of work done Off-Broadway and Off-Off-Broadway. But a lot of it is pretty bad, and much of it is fleeting and very small-scale. Set aside the question of cultural quality for a moment. The average Off-Broadway show is seen by something like 1 in 10,000 people. Even a big Broadway show plays to perhaps 10,000 people a week, while a successful TV series plays to 30 million people an episode. So the critic has a twofold problem. He has got to justify his job—to find enough work that really merits being written about. Then he has to persuade the editor that these stories are really worth printing. The general attitude in periodicals these days is: "Theater is a boutique section for us. It's not a supermarket section, not a main part of what we do."

The third basic problem is trying to find a vocabulary of criticism, a frame of reference, that makes the theater seem relevant to readers who do not go to see shows regularly. In a sense, the critic has to become part of the theatrical community and engage himself in some audience-building or at least reputation enhancement.

The fourth problem is to reconcile this more populist vocabulary with securing more knowledgeable critics. One of the problems with getting critics who are practitioners, or critics who have scholarly credentials, is that they are the ones most apt to preach only to the already converted. The trick is to find critics who can speak to a mass audience without seeming stupid and ignorant to the theater-going aficionado.

The biggest problem of the review format is that it tends just to take the work on its own terms. The basic shape of every review is: I went last night and I saw this thing; here's what happens, and here's what I think about it. What's missing from that is the sense of how this work relates to what else is going now in the arts and in society, of how it taps into personal psychological matters, of how it reveals the development of either an individual artist or an artistic school. The review format puts far too much emphasis on the consumer question: "Should I go or not go; should I spend my money or not?"

One thing that would generally improve American theater criticism is if it were more like the European model, in which criticism is written far more often by people who are in some other way practitioners. But it is not at all in keeping with the American journalistic traditions, which is like a big exercise in voting: you are supposed to be able to react the way the average person would react. Instead of lifting the audience's level of knowledge and background, you simply recreate the experience that it would have if it were to go there, and the emphasis is always more on the emotional result of one's response, rather than on the reasoning process that gets you there. To me this way of doing things is totally wrong. I've always thought that whether you've liked it or not is the least interesting part of a review. The point is to be able to understand the social, political, and artistic context out of which the work arises and to be able to explain that to the audiences.

But a great many American critics are intellectually timid. They are afraid to grapple with larger philosophical questions because they don't think they are smart enough. They won't say that out loud, but it's fairly apparent. They don't do risky things in print. I have read a lot of critics in my time and a great many of them are plainly afraid of getting caught out not knowing or not understanding. In trying to avoid making fools of themselves, they do it anyway. That's why they shouldn't be doing the job. One notable exception to this is Frank Rich: he is very venturesome as a writer and he's not afraid of ideas and interpretations. It's astonishing how quickly most critics run the other way if they see a metaphor or an analogy coming up. They want to tell you the plot, but they don't recognize what lies beneath it, how the plot stands for something else or has other ways of meaning, and frequently they just don't get it at all. I may sound extremely arrogant because I think I generally do get it. But the truth is that artists are right not to heed reviews, because most reviewers are just not smart enough to grasp what the artist already knows. There is a certain rough justice in having mediocrities as critics. If no smarter than the average audience member, they probably aren't any dumber either, and if the critics don't get it, neither will a lot of the audience. If the work of art is incomprehensible maybe the artist needs to rethink how explicit and open his work needs to be. But I still think that if the critic has any useful role to perform, it's in opening the eyes of the audience. So on balance, I prefer more brains and knowledge than my brethren generally offer.

HOLLY HILL

The major problem in criticism today is the lack of knowledge and care on the part of editors who hire critics. I don't think most editors would dare to hire somebody who didn't know anything technically about music to be a music critic, and yet they will hire theater critics without special knowledge of the theater. If somebody who doesn't know about the theater is hired to be theater critic, his or her guilt is in accepting it. How dare they do that? Would they accept a position of the sports writer if they didn't know anything about sports? No, because they realize that their readers would catch them.

Something else we have to face: women have occupied major positions in theater criticism only in the last decade. And you still don't have in mainstream publications people of color—men or women. What matters is variety. This can make criticism more interesting.

It's terribly detrimental that the theater criticism at *The New York Times* is about the only game in the town insofar making or breaking a play. And I don't see any changes in the foreseeable future because economically it's just not viable for there to be twelve newspapers.

**- As a correspondent of *The Times* of London for the New York theater, you
are the right person to make a comparison between theater criticism in
America and in England. What are the main differences and how they affect
the theater itself?**

Holly Hill: The major comparison is that there are 10 to 12 newspapers in London,
so you don't have only one, or even two or three, critics who can make or break
any given show. That's enormously healthy for the theater. Another difference is
that the British are much more accustomed to seeing classics than we are. They
are brought up with the knowledge of the classical canon that the American critics
don't have because they simply don't see it. Also, it is easier to get to the regional
theaters in Britain from London than it is to get to all of this country's theaters—
it's simply a smaller world. The critics have an opportunity to become much more
familiar with the work of actors and directors from early on and to follow them
through their careers. It's much more possible in England for young talents to be
discovered early and nurtured than it is here.

JONATHAN KALB

In one phrase: the state of American publications—that is the main problem. It has
nothing to do with the theater; it has to do with the lower expectations and standards
of the existing publications. Also, the shrinking number of publications: that's another
big aspect of the problem. Today it's an enormous privilege to be given space to
publish your opinions on any cultural event in a publication that appears frequently
enough to be on sale while the event is still running.

An acquaintance of mine—a theater critic—once filled in for the sports writer
on his paper when the sports writer was sick for a month, and the stories about
how much mail he got are incredible. If you make a mistake on a baseball player's
batting average by one hundredth of a point, you'll get six letters. If you say that
Willie Mays hit .385 in a season when he really hit .388, you'll get ten letters. But
print that "Henrik Ibsen wrote *Hamlet* during his boyhood in Tunisia," and nobody
will blink. It's not that they don't catch it; they just don't care.

It may hurt to admit it, but no one cares that much about serious thought on
theater; it just doesn't have a large readership. And that's another reason why theater
criticism in this country is in such a shabby state: bright young minds don't have
a lot of reasons to apply themselves to the field. It's beyond the problem of lacking
the rewards and accolades available to other intellectuals; the field isn't really respected
in the culture. The German critic Friedricht Luft, was the central figure of Berlin
newspaper theater reviewing after World War II,and he just died last year. On his
75th birthday, I remember there was a front-page feature article about him in the
Berliner Morgenpost, and at his death there were feature pieces in all of the major
newspapers in Germany. That man had the privilege of feeling throughout his life
that he was important to his society, that what he did mattered to the culture. This
is not the case in this country even for Frank Rich, or for whoever holds that *Times*
job. Theater criticism is a literally thankless task here, which is why I can't understand

how anybody can do it for very long if their work doesn't come from love of the form.

STANLEY KAUFFMANN

Speaking of New York, I'd say that the position of criticism has not changed in my lifetime. It's always been very influential. What has changed are two things. First, criticism has now been concentrated in a very few people. Second, the education and the depth of the critic, in theater terms, have improved a very great deal. But because critics have had that education, that doesn't mean in the long run that they are necessarily any deeper. It's quite deceptive now. In a sense it's more insidious because when you read a review by Mr. Smith in 1935, you knew he was a fool, now when you read a review by Mr. Smith 2nd, it seems intelligent: he's using a lot of long words in reference to Kafka, Dostoyevsky, Bahktin, but he doesn't perceive any more than his predecessors did. I discovered this, by the way, in connection with English criticism. I grew up reading English magazines and when I began to see some of the plays they were writing about, I understood that, by and large, they were not any brighter than the American critics, they just wrote better. That's a bit of what's happened in this country. I'd like to sum it up in terms of quality by saying that I have no very high regard for most of the critics now writing in this country.

WALTER KERR

Theater criticism used to be more colorful and more important. *The New York Times* had a lot of trouble finding a new Sunday critic now; years ago, Oh my God, you had them lined up in the streets outside around the building. The plum of the whole was the drama critics' job. You got free tickets; you had to see all the shows. The change in the media generally is the reason; movies, TV and also the nature of reviewing has changed somewhat.

HOWARD KISSEL

It's not interesting to write about a theater that's mediocre. Most of the young playwrights have a TV sensibility. They haven't seen good classical theater. They have no ear for theater dialogue. They write scripts that might be fine on the small screen but lack the depth of theater. I cannot say that I find my job stimulating or exciting, because the theater I see is neither of the above.

Arthur Miller made an interesting observation. He said that when he came into the theater in the early '40s, most of the newspaper reviewers were reporters who had a mentality like that of the people who covered fires or burglaries. Their taste was much like that of their readers. By the '60s, though, even the daily papers had critics whose orientation was academic. They were not just average reporters. They fancied themselves intellectuals. He did not feel this was a change for the better.

In a certain way he is right. There's much more pretension in theater criticism

than there used to be. If you read theater criticism of the '30s, '40s or '50s, the
tone is conversational and wonderfully descriptive, much less analytical. The writing
is vivid, like good reporting. It has a breathless quality, as if the critic has just come
from covering a four-alarm fire. By contrast most of the criticism today is very dry.
In part it's because what the critics today see is also very dry.

STEWART KLEIN

The level of criticism has decreased over the years. Too many critics today are cheer-
leaders who like to see their name in advertisements. You pick up a paper each
week and you see all these quotes, "This play is great!", "That play is great!" It's
awful! And all these people are supposed to be critics. When I first began, a marvellous
critic, Ted Kalem, took me aside and he said to me, "Young man, let me give you
some advice about what you are doing. In the entire 2000-year history of the theater,
there might be 20 plays that are masterpieces. Now your job is to go on the air
and say, "The thing that opened on Broadway tonight is not one of those 20." That
advice is still valid.

JACK KROLL

The main problem of American theater criticism has to do with something very
simple: the understanding of the editors and their attitude towards the importance
of the theater.

GLENN LONEY

The first problem is: will there be enough theater left to criticize? Then, there's
very little training of critics per se. But there's a good reason for that: where are
they going to work? The truth is that even if you get an M.A.or a Ph.D. in criticism,
do you think that the newspapers would hire a Ph.D.? No! The answer is, "The
readers are ordinary people. We don't need somebody with an advanced degree!
We are great democrats; we like the average man! Just because you know a lot,
it doesn't make you a good writer!" Sometimes editors seem to think anyone can
write about theater, "You are an educated person, just go see the play and tell
us what you thought about it." This means that reviews may be written by people
who have never read very many plays; they haven't studied history of the theater.
When a castle wall suddenly becomes transparent, and you see a ghost behind
it, they are amazed, like little children. They say, "Oh, *how* did they do that?" A
trained theater person knows perfectly well how these things are done. And I think
that innocence appalling.

I don't understand how a theater critic cannot be interested in opera. But then,
most of the Broadway musicals are reviewed by people who don't know much
about music; they review the characters and the story.

The time has come when we must train people who really love the performing
arts. We should encourage them to start going to symphonies, operas, dance, theater,
even working backstage. I don't think that you could write knowingly, even as

a reporter, unless you have understood everything about theater: its history, its machinery, its technology, the training of actors. But theater, and many other art-forms, don't seem to be "important" in American life. That's our loss. It's not that way in Europe.

DAVID RICHARDS

The general failings of criticism in America are two. Either it tends to function as a consumer guide and says, "Green light—Go!, Red light—Stop! Yellow light—take your chance!" These are the people who give out four stars or three stars. They could be talking about nylon stockings or a new muffin as easily as about a play. The other end of criticism is the academic one: it dissects theater as if it were a frog in a biology class. I think both kinds injurious.

GORDON ROGOFF

The main problem in American theater criticism is detachment from reality. It's limited to addressing art as entertainment: entertaining our readers and then in turn advising them how to be entertained. I don't think that theater is about entertainment. It should be about pleasure: pleasure derived from engagement with ideas and experience. That's what I'd hope the criticism would address. The problem is that our criticism only disconnects, it's too unengaged in a struggle to make life durable. This is its journalistic mannerism.

JOHN SIMON

There are fewer critics now than ever, either in theater or in film, or in anything else. When I say fewer, I don't mean, fewer bad ones; I mean, fewer good ones. The reason for this is not simple, and it's not necessarily the lack of potentially good critics. There are very few publications in which you can write criticism, and, out of those, many don't give you enough space. And some insist that you be positive, or at least more positive than you want to be, and that eliminates real criticism.

Then, the fact that it's so hard to make a living as a critic deters a lot of good people from going into this field. Even if you write for *The New York Times* or for some very fancy magazine, in today's world, that is not a wonderful living. Oh, you don't starve, and it's not horrible, but it's certainly not an easy life. And it's true that for a while—in the '50s or '60s—critics, especially film critics, suddenly became important in the eyes of the public, and criticism was thought to be a glamorous profession. But that attitude disappeared fairly quickly, and I don't think many people now think of being a critic as being very special or exciting. In fact, a lot of people think of criticism as an unpleasant, self-promoting, and unnecessary thing.

The other problem is that in order to be a real critic, you have to have a good education. It's almost the most important thing. And a good education is harder and harder to get.

On top of these things, there is the concept of democracy in this country, which may be politically a good one, but artistically, aesthetically, it's bad. The concept that, somehow, equality should exist in the world of the arts as well is a nonsensical notion, based on social and political considerations that are totally irrelevant to the arts. The idea that one piece of work is better than another is often considered by people who don't know any better—which means a great many people—an elitist notion. And, unfortunately, in this country the word "elitist" is a very dirty word. I myself consider it wonderful and honorable. The populace thinks that it is arrogant and stupid to think that something in art is much better than something else, because if a human being is worth just as much as the next human being, then a play is worth just as much as the next play. Which is, of course, totally wrong.

Essentially the idea in America is that the critic should really not know more about the theater than anybody else. He should just be there, and be sincere and concerned and loving, but there's no need for this person to be smarter than the others. Therefore any critic who is suspected of knowing more is treated as a swine by a lot of people, even in some cases by the people who would hire him, because eventually they don't want critics to show them up as knowing less. This is very bad, this hatred of elitism. The arts are an aristocracy. In society, in politics, we should not be aristocratic, but in the arts we must be. But people have to learn to make the distinction between art and life. That, for example, you can be the most wonderful playwright in the world, but a horrible human being, or the most wonderful human being, but a terrible playwright or critic. And that is a great problem for people: to make distinctions, not to allow personal matters to color their aesthetic judgment.

Then, people don't understand that the arts are different from news, from reportage. And that's for an obvious reason: so much criticism in America has been written as a journalistic account of what goes on in the theater, rather than as intelligent thinking about it, with understanding, erudition, and evaluation.

EDWIN WILSON

The biggest problem is that there's just not enough activity in the New York theater, both in terms of quality and quantity, not nearly as much as there was when I started 19 years ago. To get enough space to write is also always a problem.

Then, many of the people who go into criticism, particularly in the newspapers and TV, have very little background in theater. They may have had one or two courses at college, but they certainly have not taken a graduate degree in theater. That's a problem, because I don't think they are properly prepared in terms of information and experience to be the best judges of some of the things they see.

LINDA WINER

I'm afraid that, for several different reasons, the volume of theater criticism has been turned up; people are shouting more in print. There is a tendency to feed the appetite for the hit-flop mentality of the audience: that either a play is the greatest thing anybody's ever seen, or it doesn't deserve to live. In fact, most of the theater falls somewhere in between that. Sometimes I sit there and I think, "It's only a play; no one was killed!" Similarly with the ravings, "It's not going to change your life, ladies and gentlemen, it's only a play." The number of plays that has changed my life is very small, and I probably go five times a week to the theater. But this is the American mentality: America loves winners and losers, and that phenomenon really fits into it. And this is not the best of the American mentality. I don't like sports either. I'm not a scorekeeper and I don't like watching us being turned into scorekeepers.

I grew up at a time when it was embarrassing for people to want to make a lot of money; what you wanted to do was to do good work. It's certainly not the case now. I'm afraid that the style of criticism, "Who can yell louder? Who can say it funnier? Who can be meaner?" is definitely fitting right into it.

5 HEAVY LIES THE CROWN: POWER AND CRITICISM

Clive Barnes
Robert Brustein
Dennis Cunningham
Michael Feingold
Jeremy Gerard
Mel Gussow
William A. Henry III
Holly Hill
Jonathan Kalb
Stanley Kauffmann

Walter Kerr
Howard Kissel
Stewart Klein
Jack Kroll
Glenn Loney
Frank Rich
David Richards
Gordon Rogoff
John Simon
Linda Winer

They answer the questions:

- **What's your opinion/explanation of the power/influence of theater criticism and of the status of the critics as sort of "legislators" of audiences' taste?**

- **What do you think about the plea of *The Village Voice* for diminishing the critics' power?**

CLIVE BARNES

It's very difficult to understand the power of *The New York Times,* unless you are a native New Yorker. It's like a bible to New Yorkers. It takes ages to understand that and even now I understand it intellectually, but not with my heart. When I was the *Times* critic, we used to have the same kind of problems. It's an awesome responsibility. It's very unpleasant. It's not so much that plays will die by what is written about them (some do, a certain kind of plays). It's the general perception that that's true, and the pressure put on one is quite remarkable.

Now, a solution? It has been suggested that the *Times* have more than one critic, perhaps two critics. It wouldn't really make such a difference. In the first place, a lot of the notice is information, so one has to say, "Look, you tell the story this time; I'll do it next time." Otherwise, the notices would be remarkably similar. Next difficulty: within two or three weeks, one of the people would have established himself as the *Times'* critic. A third thing: New Yorkers at the present time are looking not for reasons to go to the theater, but for reasons not to go to the theater. What would happen if both critics agreed that the play is good? That might help a bit. But if both of them disagreed on it, that would be more deadly even than before. So in merely practical terms, I don't think it would work. The other thing is: why should the *Times* treat Broadway any different from everything else? Why don't they have two reviewers for a concert, a movie, a football match?

Theater costs a lot. This is another reason why the critics are powerful. But there are examples where public opinion goes absolutely against the critic. If a play can last long enough, no one will remember what the critics said about it. For example, no one knows that Frank Rich and I, and almost every critic in the town, disliked *Cats*. Now, if you ask people they'll say, "Oh, the critics loved *Cats!*" Or when I was at the *Times*, I didn't like *Jesus Christ Superstar*. What counts in the long run is word-of-mouth. If, when the producers make a play, they were compelled to put a certain amount of money in a bank account that would pay the salaries of the artists and union people for two weeks or ideally even three months, it would give the word-of-mouth a chance to circulate and build a favorable attitude among the audience. This would do much more to curb the power of the critics than having two critics on the *Times*. But producers don't like the idea because they would have to raise more money.

ROBERT BRUSTEIN

If I've done anything as a critic myself, I hope it is to persuade my readers that my opinion is as good or as bad as theirs, that there are many opinions you can have about a single production, and no one of them is right about it. I don't believe in critics telling us what we should be seeing and what we shouldn't be seeing. What the best critics do is to stimulate thought about the theater and encourage the audience just to make up their own minds.

- **You've said, that you've enjoyed "the luxury of an authoritative platform, without being shackled by the restrictions of power." What do you think the restrictions of power are in the position of Frank Rich?**

Robert Brustein: That's a terrible responsibility to know that people have been working for as much as six months or a year on a particular project and you've seen them on one night to determine whether they are going to go on working or be out of work the next day, whether the playwright is going to be respected or ridiculed, whether the actor is going to be treated as someone worthy of interest or not. This is the sort of thing that sits on your shoulders when you're being read by thousands of people who are waiting to hear whether or not they should go to the theater. These are the shackles of power.

DENNIS CUNNINGHAM

It would be a lot easier without this power. Critics would prefer this, too. But economics is what makes it a live-or-die situation and it's just that people think twice about spending their money. But I don't think critics close shows. No! Producers do, as Frank Rich says. All most care about is what *The New York Times* thinks of what they are doing. So, if they are going to pay attention to no one but the *Times,* and it hasn't liked them, they have no reason to complain. By the way, who wrote this in *The Village Voice?* I'm highly suspicious of *The Village Voice,* I stopped reading it some years ago.

MICHAEL FEINGOLD

The power is unavoidable in a city where theater tickets are so expensive and taste is untrained—because Americans really are not very well educated and cultivated at this point in time.

You cannot demolish what people believe is necessary, but it's all a matter of approach. If you use your power to control people and say, "You must think this and you must not think that," then you're using it destructively; you're programming people. On the other hand, you could use your power to open up areas people haven't thought about. Brooks Atkinson was not a great genius. *The New York Times* has only employed in its history as a paper two great drama critics: Stark Young lasted, I think, 10 weeks; Stanley Kauffmann lasted two seasons. But Atkinson was an earnest, serious-minded, decent man who didn't go around waving a machete. Consequently, although the *Times* review was the principal cue for people to buy tickets, nobody complained about Brooks Atkinson having too much power. He never went on vendettas against anyone; he used his power reasonably.

- Don't you also want to have power?
Michael Feingold: Of course, and I do have power. But I don't use it abusively. I use it to provoke people's interest in things they might like. I use it to warn them of things they might not like. The influence over the artists is a much more complex matter, because who's to say what influences artists? The influence I have seen on artists from my reviews has been minimal. But I don't ask for more than that.

JEREMY GERARD

That's a problem with no solution. As the theater becomes less and less of a cultural habit and more and more of an occasion, as it costs so much, and as there are so few new things, the critics have a tremendous amount of power. If you are affected by the knowledge of that power, you are in the wrong job. If you start writing what you perceive your readers want, or what the producers want, you are dead. In many ways criticism without power is better. One of the nice things when I worked in Dallas was that theater criticism was less powerful.

I don't think it's the critics' fault that they have power. I don't think it's *The New York Times'* fault that it's the one paper that people who go to the theater read. And were I in Frank Rich's position I would struggle, as he does, not to let it affect me. Ultimately, because we are sensitive human beings it does affect us to some greater or lesser extent, but the best critics are those who remain honest to their own vision of what is good and what's bad.

MEL GUSSOW

The power of critics is overrated. Seldom do critics close shows and then it is generally by consensus. In spite of negative notices, even in *The New York Times,* shows have continued to run. Critical power, when it exists, is more often in the area of extending the life of a play, of bringing it to the attention of a wider public.

WILLIAM A. HENRY III

Most of the critic's influence has to do with the economic circumstances in which theater work is produced. A good producer, if he spends $3 million producing a show, sets an extra $500,000 aside so that, if the reviews aren't great, he can keep the show running until the public starts to say, "Hey, you know that really isn't a bad show!" But most producers don't do that and then they say, "The critics are so powerful!" I say, "The producers are so irresponsible!" They are depending on the critic to do the producers' job, which is to sell the show. And it isn't that the critics kill the shows. The shows are dead on arrival, because of the producers' errors in judgement and neglect. Critics are expected to conjure up an audience where none existed—and, in the case of straight plays, none is normal. There is no ongoing public for serious drama, or rather, not enough of one. So, another reason for the so-called influence of critics is the precarious state of public interest. Plus, of course, ticket prices so high that people expect ecstasy rather than mere entertainment.

HOLLY HILL

If the criticism doesn't have influence, there's no point of it, except to make a historical record. I hate to think of a theater, or an art, where no one is offering a commentary on it. There's enough pretension and dumb stuff that gets out anyway. It's just a matter of achieving a balance. In the best of all possible worlds, you will have critics who are well-informed, very good writers or broadcasters, and very responsible. They won't praise to the skies something that's mediocre. And even if they hate something, they won't use the play, or the playwright, or the director, to take out some personal frustration.

In New York so many people are against the power of the criticism because it's concentrated in *The New York Times,* which is a make-or-break situation. Peter Rabbit could have the job of the *Times'* theater critic and it would still have that same power. There is a tremendous nostalgia for the days of Brooks Atkinson, who was considered to be a gentleman critic. People call Frank Rich a bully-boy. I'm not saying whether I agree with that or not, I'm just saying that is one of the points. But we must remember that Brooks Atkinson was writing at a time when Walter Kerr was also writing for *The New York Herald Tribune* and there were a lot of other critics who had some influence.

JONATHAN KALB

Most of the people who complain about critical power in the theater are people who are pissed off about some negative review in the recent past. It's utter nonsense to talk about the power of criticism in any context but *The New York Times*. To say it's a major problem elsewhere is simply not true. Sure, a good review in another publication can increase audiences; a bad one can decrease them; I don't deny that. But the claim that whole careers are made or broken by good or bad reviews— that has *only* to do with the *Times,* and even that is not so simple a process as it seems. I know actors who got their big breaks due bad reviews in the *Times.*

STANLEY KAUFFMANN

You can't talk about the influence of critics in plural. It's *The New York Times'* review for Broadway that makes or breaks the show, and that's a dreadful position to be in. No sane and responsible critic wants that influence. You don't become a critic to have the influence of a hangman.

WALTER KERR

We'd be much happier without power. Then you can write anything you want. It has always made me a little troubled. There's always that fear of having too much power, of being somewhat guilty. There was a fine character actor who lived across the street from us. Once he was doing a play called *The First Gentlemen*. I had to go and cover it. The show was not very good; he was all right. You have to swallow that and to write the review. Then we came home. But driving down our street, my wife—Jean said, "I feel badly for Walter, poor Walter." And I said, "Maybe Brooks will like it!" That's the psychology.

HOWARD KISSEL

If critics have power, it stems from the fact that New York no longer has a theater audience who cares about the theater. In London if there is a new Pinter or Ayckbourn play, regardless of what the reviewers say, people want to see it. We have killed off those theatergoers. In New York the only people who are knowledgeable about theater are people who started going 40 or 50 years ago, whose habit is so ingrained that even the mediocre, lackluster plays they see cannot kill their appetite.

Nowadays people seem to go to the theater not because they want to be stimulated or moved, but because in some way it enhances their status to be able to say they saw X or Y. There's too little pleasure in what's being produced for anyone to go on a regular basis on any rational grounds. They wait for the shows that are chic, which over the last few years have tended to be the big British musicals.

As for *The Village Voice,* they still buy the myth of the avant-garde. On the rare occasions I read it, I always have the feeling I have entered a room where everyone is screaming. The writers throughout the paper tend to be leftists who have become more hysterical now that no one with any sense takes leftist ideas very seriously.

They must imagine the volume of their voices compensates for the hollowness of what they have to say. They have the passion of fanatics, absolutely convinced they are in possession of the truth about everything—politics, books, movies, the theater. They still nurture the notion that we have a great, adventurous experimental theater that is constantly pushing forward boundaries.

The man who wrote the article you mentioned is convinced he's leading an army into unknown territory. On the horizon he sees an enemy, which he perceives as inimical to the progressive forces he is leading. He sees *The New York Times* as an obstacle to the success of his forces, though in fact the *Times* is actually on his side more often than he's willing to acknowledge.

Nevertheless it's part of the rhetoric of the left that the bourgeoisie is thwarting the avant-garde. The *Times,* as an essentially bourgeois voice, must be inveighed against.

As for power, even the *Times* is limited. It depends on the producers and the money they have at their disposal to publicize a show or just keep it open. In 1989 a play called *A Few Good Men* opened. Especially in the initial production, the flaws of the play were apparent, and the *Times* gave it an extremely negative review. But it was a play the audience loved, and word-of-mouth kept it running for more than a year despite the *Times* review. The *Times,* quite rightly, gave a negative review to *Cats.* It's about to celebrate its 10th birthday. Of course there are also little plays, that might be overlooked, that a supportive *Times* review can help. Caryl Churchill's *Mad Forest* is a good example.

As I said earlier, if we had a true theater audience, the press would not matter. The *cognoscenti* would support the work that deserves support.

STEWART KLEIN

The fact of the matter is: if a play is good, it'll run, and if it's not good, it will not run. If you have a lousy play and a thousand critics out of a thousand critics write, "This play is wonderful theater," that'll help the play for a week or two. But every audience that sees that play will come out and say, "What are those stupid critics talking about? This play is terrible," and they'll tell their friends, and it'll take no time at all for the word to get around. That's always what sells or kills a play. You can't disguise a bad play or a good play. It stands on its own . There was that *60 minutes* program about Frank Rich, which was one of the silliest and most fallacious pieces of journalism I've ever seen, where they called him "the butcher of Broadway" and accused him of destroying Broadway. That is simply not true. What is killing Broadway is Broadway: you put on lousy plays and charge horrendously escalating prices—who's going to go?

JACK KROLL

The reasons for the critics' influence? You cannot start with anything else but economics, when you get these letters from people saying, "I took your advice and went to see this play. It was a total waste of money and you owe me $130."

The critics' influence is also part of a more general phenomenon which has to do with the impact of the media. Reading newspapers and magazines has become a media-experience. You are reading Frank Rich, or Jack Kroll—and it's a person who's talking. It's fun to connect with another human being. That's a tremendously enjoyable experience.

There's one more important reason and it's a cliche: there's too much out there; you are constantly bombarded by so many things even if you don't want to know about them. It's confusing; it's very difficult to sort it out. The critic is a kind of a guide through a maze, through a very complicated universe.

GLENN LONEY

I would say Frank Rich doesn't close plays. They say, "the Butcher of Broadway!" They've said that about Clive Barnes, about every critic who was at *The New York Times* for the last 20 or 30 years. Producers close plays. They read the *Times* and they say, "Oh my God, the *Times* didn't like it! Let's close it." This is insane, because a lot of people who go to the theater—especially those who go to popular comedies or glitzy musicals—don't even subscribe to the *Times*. They wouldn't even know about its review, unless producers put it outside the theater. Frank Rich is very intelligent and very clever, but his high standards have been unrealistic. He wants a theater of perfection, which is impossible in our time. But there are times when he has liked a show a lot, and the public has not. A favorable *Times'* review cannot save a show, when people don't want to see it.

FRANK RICH

The reason for that influence has not to do only with theater or theater criticism. It has to do with the whole American commercialization of everything. The fact is that people don't buy a toaster without reading a review of it, or cars, or books, or anything. So theater, sadly, is not able to escape this. It's the whole mercantile ethic of this country. I don't like it. Which is not to say that I believe that socialism is the answer either. There's something tragic about the commercial system for the arts here. But that's the way this country has always been. That's the American character. You can criticize it and fight it, or try to ameliorate it, but to change it? Forget it! The fascinating other side of it is that sometimes the huge commercial pressures and big money in American art miraculously produce something great. The most notable example is Hollywood. And the truth is that, for all the junk that has been produced by the commercial theater, it also did produce *Cat on a Hot Tin Roof, Death of a Salesman* and *Long Day's Journey into Night*. That doesn't justify the system, but it's fascinating that sometimes in spite of everything, art comes out of it. I'm constantly amazed when there's a great Hollywood movie, or a musical like *My Fair Lady* on Broadway.

As for diminishing the power of the critics, first of all, there is free speech or there isn't. It's simple. The power of the critic is only to the extent that people read the critic, trust the critic and are convinced by the critic's beliefs. That's what

free speech is all about. That's also the right of the playwright to use the power
of the stage. Brooks Atkinson, the *Times* drama critic before I was born, said, "The
only real power in the theater is the power of a good play on the stage." If censorship
is applied to one group of writers, it could be applied to all groups of writers.
It's putting the fox into chicken coop. So the diminishing of the critic's power is
a diminishing of freedom of speech. And frankly, the critics get power only because
of their talent, and the playwrights get power only because of *their* talent. In a
free society, the public is the final arbiter; if people don't want to believe a critic,
believe me, they won't. There have been critics of the *Times* who have failed very
quickly, because they didn't have the trust of the readers.

DAVID RICHARDS

Maybe the chief reason is that it's too much of an investment of money. People
want some reassurance that their money and their time are not going to be misspent.
But usually it's not the power of the critic; it's the power of the publication. It's
very simple: if my reviews did not appear in that newspaper and were printed on
· a piece of paper instead and I were handing them out on the street corner, they
would not have a great deal of importance. When I was at the *Washington Star,*
it was the less powerful of the two papers in the town. So for my first 12 years
as a critic, I didn't have the power of the critic of the *Washington Post*. When I
went to *The Washington Post,* nothing changed: my personality, my writing, my
taste remained the same. The only thing that changed was the newspaper I was
working for, and the difference was enormous. But that was, I thought, a good
thing to happen, because I quickly realized that it was never my power.

GORDON ROGOFF

I don't want power; I'd rather have influence than power. I don't want to affect
whether a work will find an audience or not. I don't want my role to be to advise
foundations, "Don't support this artist!" Yet I know that that's the way it operates,
which makes me feel quite uneasy.

JOHN SIMON

There are not many influential drama critics in this country. First of all, if you are
not in New York—and even if you are in New York, but write for one of the less
popular publications—nobody knows you. For example, nobody reads my film
criticism, because almost nobody interested in film reads the *National Review*. On
the other hand, if you think how big this country is, how many magazines it has
or could have, how many influential critics it could have and doesn't have. Well,
it's a sobering thought.

    The power of the critic is never that great. And when it is, it's accidental. The
only critic in the theater who has any power as an individual is the *New York Times's*
No. 1 critic. And even that power has now been considerably diminished because

of the prevalence of TV reviewing, which is an insanity beyond compare. But there, again, it's not the power of one TV critic, but of all of them together.

LINDA WINER

I don't want to hear from the producers, "This is a one-newspaper town," because they are the ones who end up channeling stories to one newspaper. I don't want to hear from them, "Critics have so much power," because they end up using our quotes. If the producers don't want the critics to have power, then they don't have to use quotes in their ads. You can't really play both sides.

The answer is more voices. Then it becomes less a matter of who can kill a show, and more a matter of having bubbles in the air about the theater. Sometimes I go to something and I think, "That's not my kind of a show, but I know that there's a huge audience. My parents, for example, might have liked it. How am I to say that it should be kicked because it isn't my kind of a show?" It's a tricky thing. You can't write reviews in someone else's head, but these are times when you have, sort of, to say, "This is what it is. For what it is trying to do, it does it. It wouldn't be my choice, but..."

6 THE LIVE-OR-DIE FACTOR: DESTRUCTIVE AND CONSTRUCTIVE CRITICISM

Dennis Cunningham
Howard Kissel
David Richards

Joel Siegel
Edwin Wilson
Linda Winer

They answer the questions:

- Do you think about criticism in terms of being constructive or destructive? What are your ideas in this respect?

- Do you think criticism needs to be supportive in order to keep theater alive?

DENNIS CUNNINGHAM

It's awfully hard to be constructively critical in a minute and 45 seconds. You are essentially there to describe and say, "Yes!" or "No!", and try to do it as honestly and open-heartedly as possible. Then, even destructive criticism implies constructiveness. It implies some ideal, and sometimes things are so awful and misbegotten.

I don't agree that criticism should be supportive just for the sake of support. But, there should not be this "us" and "them" mentality. On the other hand, we have a real obligation to the audience, and it would be idiotic in order to keep the theater alive to say, "You might enjoy this!" at $60 a ticket! That's misguided to pretend that things are better than they actually are, and I don't think it does anybody any favour.

HOWARD KISSEL

Theater people who complain that theater critics are not "supportive" enough generally mean they're not supportive enough of the work those particular people are doing. When they say we should be more constructive, they mean we should encourage readers to see their work. I don't think it benefits anyone to send readers to work I think is shoddy, however full it is of good intentions. That's how we've killed the audience over the years. We've sent them to a lot of phoney, second-rate plays that, for one reason or another, we thought we should support.

During the '60s, when there was a lot of experimental garbage, the audience was encouraged to see this or that because it would broaden or instruct them; it would shake them of their moral torpor, etc., etc. Mainly these plays bored them, and they stopped going to the theater. I think we're still living with the legacy of that kind of "constructive" criticism.

DAVID RICHARDS

That's generally theater people who tell you that, right? They say, "Oh, why can't critics be more constructive?" Well, there is excellence and there isn't excellence; excellence should be encouraged and the lack of excellence should not be spared. I do not know why we would make an exception in the theater. If you needed a dentist, and someone said, "This dentist is pretty good, but he's not the best!", would that be OK with you? What about a plumber? If he could do 75 per cent of the job, would you hire him? You wouldn't. But when it comes to the arts, we are supposed to encourage them, indulge them. I once wrote an article in Washington that angered many actors because I said, "It's one of the few areas where people certify themselves." Nothing prevents you from saying, "I'm an actor and therefore my efforts should be encouraged!" My response would be, "Prove it to me!" But self-certification seems to be the rule in the arts; it certainly isn't the way of doctors or mechanics . There's a rigorous body of knowledge and skill, that has to be acquired; then they can say, "I'm a doctor! I'm a mechanic!" But if you have a vague artistic impulse, you think, "Oh, I feel in my soul, I'm an actor!"; you call yourself an actor from the start. Well, then along come people like the critics and say, "It seems to me that you are not an actor!" Then the poor would-be actor whimpers, "Why are you being destructive?"

JOEL SIEGEL

I would rather be positive than negative. I can be very mean and cruel, and a lot of times it's a revenge for someone who makes you spend two hours sitting through a terrible movie, for example. But I try very hard to aim my criticism at the people who are responsible and at the people who can withstand criticism. If there's an actor or an actress in a play who's just not very good, I try not to single them out. The criticism must aim at the star. I know this from my own experience.

EDWIN WILSON

Clearly, I'm in favour of constructive rather than destructive criticism. When critics attack artists too viciously, it's not helpful. If you feel that the enterprise is really insidious, invidious; if you feel that the playwright is preaching or advocating something that you think is really quite harmful, then obviously you have the right to attack them as strongly as you want to. But if you simply disapprove of an actor's performance or a director's work—and it's well intended, but just is not successful—you should say that it's not successful, but to be destructive—No! You should try to explain why it's not successful and point out to the ways it could be improved. Then, it seems to me that there is a big difference between being clever and witty and being really destructive.

LINDA WINER

We can be destructive even when we are writing positive reviews. But it comes down to the fact that I like to write criticism, and the people who've hired me like me to write criticism. We are paid to say things that you don't say in polite society. We let people in on conversations they are not supposed to be hearing. We are saying what we really think and so much of the social energy is not what people really think. Maybe that's the most interesting thing about criticism.

7 ARE THE LIAISONS DANGEROUS? (FRIENDSHIPS AND CRITICISM)

Dennis Cunningham
Michael Feingold
Jeremy Gerard
William A. Henry III
Holly Hill
Jack Kroll
Pia Lindstrom

Glenn Loney
Frank Rich
David Richards
John Simon
Alisa Solomon
Edwin Wilson
Linda Winer

They answer the question:

- **Do you think critics should refrain from being friends with theater people?**

DENNIS CUNNINGHAM

There should be a constant "give-and-take" and "back-and-forth" between the two communities. But a lot of theater people view critics as "the enemy." So I don't think it's the critics' fault at all. Critics would prefer the opposite.

JEREMY GERARD

No critic would last at any paper of integrity if he had close associations with the theater. A theater critic who thinks he is a part of the theater community is in the wrong job—that's my feeling. I have a few friendships that have developed over the years, fewer than five. If these people are involved in a show, I won't review it. On the whole, the dangers of being very involved in the theater are greater than the benefits.

MICHAEL FEINGOLD

Why should you refrain from being friends with artists? The interesting challenge is when you have to say that an artist you know has done bad work. And if you start with the assumption that all artists are innately your friends, it teaches you a great deal about how you should write. Anyone who's creating art is inherently a possible friend, and therefore good. So when I see something bad I say, "Ah, my good friend, you did a bad thing there!" and the tone is different than if I think of them as strangers or enemies. In that sense there should be much more relating between critics and artists.

WILLIAM A. HENRY III

American journalism has a tradition of standing apart from one's news subjects, to the point that a great many critics don't talk to playwrights, directors, and so on. That really disservices the purpose. For one thing, standoffish critics never get any guidance from the artists about what was in the artist's mind. This sad business comes about because critics want to be honest journalists, which is to say they don't want to be compromised; they want to give the authentic experience of just coming and seeing, and describing the work. This is a misplaced romantic ideal. In addition, frankly, it's very easy. A great many critics say, "No, a critic shouldn't be doing interviews and shouldn't be associated with the artist, because it corrupts the critic in some way." But deep down they are really thinking, "Boy, it's a pretty easy job to go to the theater four nights a week for two or three hours and then write a little piece about one or more of them. There are lots of harder ways to earn your bread. And having to go to interview all these people and synthesize more work would be one of the ways to make it harder." They don't want to do that to themselves.

I don't oppose the idea of doing interviews with artists in the least. I don't want to talk to a director about what he's attempting to accomplish before I see the play, because then I'll have no way of judging whether I would have got it on my own. But I see no harm in talking to the director after I've seen the play and before I write about why something was or wasn't done. That's just extra added information for the reader.

HOLLY HILL

One of the problems with American criticism is the philosophy that critics should not be a part of whatever artistic community they are criticizing; that they should not know anybody in their community; in fact, that knowing people may create a conflict of interest. In England, it's not that way at all. I have been to parties at English theater critics' homes where there have been actors, playwrights, directors. It was simply not a big deal and it was taken for granted that, when the critic had to go to the theater and write about a person who was at the party, that's not an ethical problem.

JACK KROLL

When my piece on *Godfather III* appeared in the magazine, I got several calls to do interviews on radio and TV. One call came from a radio station in Los Angeles. One of their questions was: how come I did this story and not David Ansen—our film critic based in Los Angeles. After that, I realized that they were saying the same old thing: Frank Copola is a friend of yours. I've known him for 20 years, but he's not a friend of mine; he's somebody whom I've known. I've known Robert de Niro for 12, 13 years; Woody Allen, but they are *not* friends. They are people whom you know because I've got to work with them.

Something has happened in America now. George J. Nathan was the closest friend of O'Neill. He had no compunctions in writing about him. Indeed, his friendship with O'Neill gave him a unique insight into him. Those meetings are terribly valuable. But we are working now in such a corrupt system, especially in the arts. Certain reporters will boast of the fact that they have access to people like senators, but Copola—"Wow! This is corrupt!"

PIA LINDSTROM

I don't go to parties after the theater or to movie parties. It's too awkward because how could you go to a party and then say you don't like them. I can't do that and I don't try.

GLENN LONEY

The critics shouldn't know all these theater people, some people tell me. If you do, how could you then write frankly about something which you didn't like? They are talking as if the only thing which a critic does is to find fault. Criticism in the United States, and even in England, has this negative aspect. He is a critic; that means that he is nasty. Nobody speaks of a critic as being somebody with high standards and knowledge, who helps us to appreciate things. It's a danger, they say, to know people of the business socially, because you won't have the courage to write about something you didn't like. I say, "Try me!" It's a matter of *how* you say it. That's a thing you have to live with. And maybe you do lose some friends. But I like talking to playwrights and other artists; you can learn things about their ideas and talents which may not have come across on stage in a particular production. It's good to call them friends and share insights into plays and performances. And it's possible to note in a critique how and why something intended did not work without vilifying them. I was fond of Alan Schneider, but sometimes he'd sulk for six months if I said something negative in a review. Later, he'd say, "You were right."

FRANK RICH

It's better in the whole of journalism to keep these two things separate. If I were a friend of George Bush and his family I don't think I should be covering the White

House for *The New York Times,* or writing editorials. The same things are true even on much lesser levels — for example, theater. I care about the theater, I care about the audience, and I care about the theatrial community, and I feel I should be fair, and I should be honest. That's why I should stay away from the theatrical community and not have favorites in it by being part of it. I have a couple of friends in the theater who were friends of mine before I was a theater critic. I just don't review them.

DAVID RICHARDS

When you have a personal knowledge of people involved in a production, you tend to see things in their performance that the uninitiated spectator isn't going to see. Let's say I know you well; I know that when you flick your hair like this, you are really nervous inside. For somebody who doesn't know you, you are just pushing your hair back. Then I see you in a play and you start flicking your hair, and I read all sort of things into the gesture. I think, "Oh, it's magnificent, what she's doing! Look at her!" And the person next to me says, "What ever are you talking about?" That's the danger of watching friends. You end up seeing something *That isn't There* for anybody else.

JOHN SIMON

I've always felt that it would be stupid to deny yourself the pleasure of being friends with a talented person. I've been friends with some directors, playwrights, filmmakers, actors, but they are always people whom I've admired, so that chances were I could quite honestly give them good reviews. However, when I do review somebody I know, I try to be more, rather than less, strict. And if the person in question is not an enlightened or generous person, he or she has resented it, even quite bitterly, and in such cases friendship stopped either permanently or for a while. If that happens, you say, "It's too bad!" But you have to live with it. It's the other person's privilege to dislike and reject you.

ALISA SOLOMON

For me it's important to know people in the theater and to talk to them, to keep up with their work and to know what they are thinking. It would be a liability to be completely detached. Theater is not something laid on a dissection table, it's a living, breathing thing. In an ideal world, critics would go to rehearsals. The whole model that the play rehearses, it has an opening night, the critic comes at the opening night, writes about the play within the next 12 hours, and that's it - it's ridiculous. How can you expect anyone to write anything thoughtful under these circumstances? On the other hand, if I asked to go to a rehearsal, the only way I would be permitted would be if I were writing some kind of a preview feature article and even then there would be a lot of anxiety. Sometimes, when I go to a new play, I ask for a copy of the script, and theaters often don't want to give it to me. It's astonishing! I have to be very insistent. I really don't understand what it is they are trying to protect. I once went to a performance and afterwards I greeted some of the performers and one of them took me aside and put her hands around my throat, in a theatrical way, shook me back and forth and said, "This is what we do to critics!" It was very upsetting to me. It was meant as a joke, but it didn't feel like a joke. On the other hand, the Obies is a time when it actually feels like there's a theater community and we are still part of it, and that tension between theater critics and theater-makers is a little bit loosened, and there is an acknowledgement that what we all want is good theater.

I work sometimes as a dramaturg, less often now than I used to do. So I get to know people in the theater and I think it's important for critics to have some working knowledge. I don't write about my friends. That's a conflict of interest. If I'm asked to review something and I know somebody in it, I ask myself, "If I hate this production, will I be able to say so?" And if the answer is "No," then I don't take the assignment. It's not that I don't trust my own critical ability. I can say if something has failed, even if it's made by a friend. The real question for me is, "Do I have the real courage to say so in print?" And even when I do, it still appears like a conflict of interest: if the public knows that I'm familiar with somebody, they might not trust that, so it's best to avoid it and get somebody else to review it.

EDWIN WILSON

Inevitably you get to know people from the theater. I don't socialize a great deal with people in the profession, but I do have friends—just through the years, for one reason or other—a few producers, playwrights, directors.

It could be dangerous. I know that in different countries there are different practices—there are advantages and disadvantages both ways. The disadvantage is that you do become friendly with certain people and it becomes very difficult to be objective when you criticize, and you really have a conflict of interest. But the advantage is that you may know what people are trying to do and understand the process about that.

LINDA WINER

I find it very difficult to be friends with theater people. It's hard enough to have an honest reaction, considering all the complicated things that go into a performance and my reaction to it, without my thinking about the feelings of the performers. I fear emotional conflicts of interest, which are probably much more insidious than the economic conflicts of interest. At the *Chicago Tribune*, critics did a lot more interviews with people they were writing about and I used to do that, but I would find that, if when I went back to the typewriter I could see a little face above it, I was in trouble. I would start to think: was I playing favorites? And maybe I'd start to be more negative, because I wanted to prove to myself I wasn't playing favorites. And it turned out to be not fair to them because maybe I would have liked it that much anyway. I'm much too emotional a person to shut down those things. But you have to have contacts. It's a mistake to isolate yourself so much that you really don't know what's going on. And if there's a time when I have to review someone with whom I have some kind of an emotional thing at all, I have the luxury of having another critic on the staff—Jan Stuart—to do it. I'd like to keep things as clean as possible.

8 THE OBJECT OF DESIRE: AMERICAN THEATER— —ITS PRESENT

Clive Barnes
Robert Brustein
Dennis Cunningham
Jeremy Gerard
Mel Gussow
William A. Henry III

Howard Kissel
Stewart Klein
Edith Oliver
Gordon Rogoff
Alisa Solomon

They answer the question:

- **What do you think about the American theater today?**

CLIVE BARNES

One of the things I hate about the American theater is its reliance on the purely contemporary. It shocks me that nearly 90 per cent of what you see here is created in the last two or three years. That strikes me as a terrible thing. There's a lack of classic theater: Sheridan, Shakespeare, Wilde, Shaw. When they are done, they are not done in an appropriate way. The explanation is that Americans have a great love for novelty. They confuse the classics with revival. Critics have not helped a lot in this respect. The older generation were very anticlassical. And the present one tends to be sophisticated: when someone starts to do classics, they say, "Well, it's not as good as Comedie Francaise, or as the British National Theater." It's true, of course, that things start small. In my lifetime, I saw the birth of the English classic theater and I know that it started very badly. The Old Vic, which is so revered in this country now, wasn't all that good, but out of that came a National Theater.

ROBERT BRUSTEIN

American theater is on the verge of some sort of a Rennaissance. We have probably as many brilliant people in acting, directing, playwriting, design, as we have ever

99

had in history. But they are not finding institutions to produce what they are doing. So we may either be on the brink of a Rennaissance or at the end of the whole thing. I don't know which, but I hope it's the first.

DENNIS CUNNINGHAM

We, in New York, had to see the decline of the theater on Broadway, but if you look around, there's still very interesting stuff going on Off-Broadway and Off-Off-Broadway, and there are thriving theaters throughout America. So the theater is more alive than it has ever been, in that sense. It just isn't focused on Broadway the way it used to be. But most people pay attention to Broadway; anything that happens on it is somehow national news, for some reason that escapes me. We've just watched that play—*Dancing at Lubnasa*. If that's not a big success, Broadway is in a big trouble, because that's a phenomenally beautiful play. We'll just see. I have a feeling it's still possible to fail despite raves from everywhere. There was a lady next to me who said at the end, "There are too many words!" That's really one thing that TV has killed—attention-spans.

So I don't feel down about anything, except I'm worried about Broadway, but they are just putting themselves out of business.

JEREMY GERARD

American theater is at the mercy of terrible economic conditions—both the subsidized theater and the commercial one. But I think that the '80s saw the birth of some of the best American writers—August Wilson, Beth Henley, Terrence McNally. There's a lot of very, very good work being done.

MEL GUSSOW

That's an enormous question. It is difficult to give a brief answer. It is also difficult not to be pessimistic. Because of the economics of theater, producers are wary of doing anything different. They resort to past formulas. A shrinkage in public and private funding for non-profit theaters has also discouraged experimentation. Some of our best writers are writing screenplays. On the other hand, theater has expanded around the country. It is no longer isolated and insulated. It has been true for many years that the regional theater is our national theater. From it are coming many of our most talented artists. There is life in the theater, but we have to search for it.

WILLIAM A. HENRY III

It used to be, when I was a boy, that there'd be 80 productions a year on Broadway. There were years when there were close to 200 in this century. But TV and film have eroded a good deal of the audience. That's not all bad. Many of the things that used to be produced on Broadway are very similar to things that are far better done on TV: light comedies, sex farces, preaching issue-dramas. Clive Barnes, who is very smart and very nice, was on a radio show with me some months ago, and he ventured the opinion that the quality of the work on Broadway, these days, is actually much higher than it used to be when Broadway was far stronger and more of a force. What's been left out, he argued, is mostly the second-rate—the ordinary and pleasant enough but unspectacular show—while you have the same small number of really fine, memorable pieces of work as in the average season of the past. If most years don't bring a new *Glass Menagerie,* well, you usually didn't have it back then either. There's a tendency to assume that because work isn't so great at the moment, it's all terrible and the end is nigh. I tend to agree with Clive that there's been a valid calling out. Probably one in three of the works produced in any given season is to some extent meritorious, and that's better than a good batting average in baseball. On the other hand, Broadway doesn't have the national resonance that it did have 50 years ago. Part of the reason we don't have an O'Neill or a Miller, or a Williams is that it's almost impossible to be an O'Neill or a Miller, or a Williams in the theater today, because the medium itself just doesn't have the same impact on the cultural life of the country.

HOWARD KISSEL

Whereas 30 years ago New York was the theatrical capital of the world, now that honor is held by London. We've become a kind of cultural backwater. We occasionally have interesting plays, but by and large our theater is mediocre. We cannot do classics very well. You tend to see gimmicky Shakespeare, lifeless Chekhov, turgid, shallow Ibsen. Whereas 30 years ago there were a lot of very interesting new plays— Arthur Miller and Tennessee Williams were still turning out extremely good plays; even Thornton Wilder was writing lovely one-acts—we have very little that's comparable, very few playwrights with ideas. Occasionally we get an interesting play—John Guare's *Six Degrees of Separation* is an example. But most of what we see is not very interesting or stimulating. There is of course the experimental theater, which has its own audience. But no matter what you give them, that audience is pleased with it because their idea of theater-going is very self-congratulatory. The artists think they are very daring, and the audience thinks it's very daring to accept the often contemptuous tone the artists take toward them. I agree with Paul Valery who said, "Everything changes, except the avant-garde." The kinds of things they did 30 years ago they're still doing.

Much is made of the growth of regional theater over the last 30 years. It's true that there are now major theaters that provide work for actors and writers all over the country. Most of these theaters, I'm afraid, are no less mediocre than the resident companies in New York. With some exceptions, many of these theaters are still oriented toward New York. They present new plays by essentially New York writers in the hope that the production will transfer to New York and they will receive royalties from a Broadway production, which will be an enormous help to them in reducing their annual deficits. This will be increasingly the case as the National Endowment for the Arts, which nurtured these regional companies, has less and less money to continue subsidizing them.

Why has our theater declined so precipitously? Part of it is our inability to hold
to standards. One symptom is our eagerness to take classical plays and reduce them
to the trivial level of our own broken society.

You can't entirely blame the young writers. They have only a shallow understanding
of what theater can do and—in a society that is dedicated to making life easy and
comfortable—a shallow understanding of life itself.

Television has had a great deal to do with the decline of our standards. To begin
with, it's a medium that encourages a passive response on the part of the viewer.
The only thing that should really galvanize the viewer is the commercials. Furthermore,
nowadays people don't seem to make the distinctions between what they see on
the screen and live actors. They talk during plays. They bring the passivity they're
used to at home into the theater. There seems to be no emotional participation
in the theater experience. When you are watching a good play, you feel the energy
going back and forth between the stage and the audience. You seldom feel that
energy these days.

STEWART KLEIN

We are in a downside in theater now, at least on Broadway. The quality and quantity
of plays have really fallen in the 25 years since I've been doing reviews. The last
couple of years have just been dreadful. Many of the shows that now win Tony
Awards wouldn't have been nominated 25 years ago. Also, a lot of the great writers
who used to write for the theater no longer do so. And it's just sad: theater now
in America is dominated by these huge English musicals, and to me they are mostly
about scenery, they are not about feelings, about people.

EDITH OLIVER

The theater is starting up again. People are very interested again. And there are
always wonderful playwrights coming up, there's always Wendy Wasserstein, and
David Mamet and Sam Shepard and August Wilson.

GORDON ROGOFF

The theater right now is at its lowest stage. It's boring. Its problem is that it dresses
up theatrical events in the United States as if they have something to say. But most
productions are quite inferior and imitative of whatever they've read about that's
going on in Europe. You can almost guess: if The Royal Shakespeare produces
an old play one year, you know that the next year it's scheduled in Texas or California,
and that'll be their idea of something innovative.

ALISA SOLOMON

American theater is in crisis as always. Broadway is irrelevant, as far as I'm concerned.
The regional theaters have gotten kind of suffocated on their subscription series:
they are so afraid of losing their audiences, that they keep doing the same things

over and over. Experimental theater has been squeezed by real estate and other financial matters, and the lack of newspapers. But I'm not terribly pessimistic. The way we think about the theater has to change. Interesting things are happening; we just don't know where to look for them. It's happening in communities, not in the big show-biz places. Theaters have been closing all over the country. The reason is that they use the corporate model from big business for their management structure—board of directors, president, and so on—and they've become so focussed on maintaining their financial legitimacy that they stopped focussing on art. They are only going to be resuscitated if they throw away their corporate model and just go back to making theater.

9 AMERICAN THEATER CRITICISM: THE FORECAST

Dennis Cunningham   **Mel Gussow**
Michael Feingold   **Jack Kroll**
Jeremy Gerard   **Linda Winer**

They answer the question:

- **What do you think the future of American theater criticism is?**

DENNIS CUNNINGHAM

I'm not terribly optimistic. Things have gotten such a mass appeal now, so it's not the time for critics to go away; it's the time for them to be better than ever. There's such a glut of entertainment that people really need guidance, not the "live-and-die" guidance, but some kind of guidance from six or seven directions. It's helpful in many ways, so I guess it's going to be around for a while.

MICHAEL FEINGOLD

The future of theater criticism? Good in other cities, less good in this one. On the other hand, there are a lot of bright young people.
- **Are you inclined to move to another city then?**
Michael Feingold: No. I intend to stay here and continue to make theater and criticism, and do both to the best of my ability. I may even be starting a theater company. I've always thought that if I ever did start a theater of my own, I would begin by getting a subscription audience, cultivate that audience, and never bother to invite the reviewers. If they want to buy a ticket and come and write, they would be welcome, but I wouldn't pay any attention to that. The great American actor William Gillette was a very celebrated star in his time and got wonderful reviews. His managers always used to say, "Why don't you use quotes from the reviews in your ads?" And he would say, "It's beneath my dignity to link myself to these people and give *them* the benefit of *my* prestige." So I would like to see reviewing removed altogether from the concept of favorable quotes. I'd like to see the audience

read the notice in the paper and say, "This interesting artist is doing a play that sounds interesting. I want to go and see it." Or possibly, they'll read a review and say, "This sounds like an interesting subject for a play."

JEREMY GERARD

There will be fewer and fewer voices. There will be more critics in the electronic media of less and less value because criticism on TV and on radio is ephemeral. We'll see more and more of that sort of capsule reviews. The venues for serious criticism will become fewer and fewer.

MEL GUSSOW

With the closing of newspapers, there are fewer places to practice criticism. The fact that this is not a growing profession reflects the nature of theater today; the more theaters that go out of business, the fewer critics will be working. When I speak to students interested in becoming theater critics, I suggest they think about some allied art or profession.

JACK KROLL

Despite everything negative I've said about American theater criticism, I think the best critical minds for the last couple of generations and at the moment are in fact Americans. There's something about the best kind of American criticism that is extremely special, and that is: a new quality of mind and of sensibility, a mixture of intelligence and taste which I don't really see in a lot of European countries. That started to happen in the '20s and has continued up to the present. So I'm optimistic.

LINDA WINER

The more we play into what's already in the society and feed the hit-and-flop mentality, and train people to want more and more of this sensationalistic plus-minus business, that only leads to wanting more. I'm afraid that I really don't see the criticism getting less noisy. But I'm not very good at looking into the future.

Part III
Intermission With A Smile:
12 Curious Stories From The Critics' Professional Lives

SWEET IS FAME

Clive Barnes

The critic is taken terribly seriously in this country. He becomes a kind of celebrity, which is really funny. Although people don't come up to you so much in New York, once you leave New York and go to London, for example, if the American tourists recognize you, it's like seeing someone from home. I remember an occasion after I had been *The New York Times'* critic for about five years. I was in London at The Royal Shakespeare Company and, although I don't like the first nights with the flashes of the cameras, I happened to be at a first night, and I found myself sitting with all my English colleagues who, of course, knew me. There were a lot of Americans in the audience. Some American students spotted me and they came running up to ask me to sign their programs. Without thinking, I started doing it and soon there was a line of people. I signed and signed. My former English colleagues found this so funny and I saw them all roaring with laughter. I suddenly realized how ridiculous it was for a critic to be signing theater programs. What the hell had the critic to do with that? Nothing showed me so clearly the difference between the English attitude and the American attitude to criticism. It means that some critics here take themselves very seriously. And the critics are the least important people in the theater. They are just commentators; they are parasites.

IF PLAYWRIGHTS WERE IN CHARGE OF CRITICS' LIVES

Mel Gussow

Once at a dinner party I was seated next to a playwright. In the middle of our conversation, I started to choke. Noticing my distress, the playwright leaped to her feet and applied the Heimlich maneuver. Oddly, no one else at the table noticed. She saved my life. This, I submit, was a singular event in the relationship between critics and playwrights. I recounted that story in an article in *The New York Times* and I said I would not name the playwright for fear of ruining her reputation in the eyes of other playwrights. I added that it was unlikely she would ever receive a bad review from this critic. In the mail came a letter from someone signing herself "Woman Playwright." Speaking as a reader of my reviews and "as a victim of one of them," she said that I was lucky not to have been sitting next to her at that dinner. If so, she said, "I would have let you choke and take my chances with your successor." I have that letter posted on my bulletin board warning me of the perils of my profession.

WHAT CAN TURN A CRITIC INTO A 14-YEAR-OLD NERD

Holly Hill

I went to the Guthrie Theater two years ago to see a production of *Hamlet* starring the Yugoslavian-American actor Zeljko Ivanek. I had seen him and I have been an admirer of him in such works as *Loot* at the Manhattan Theater Club; he's been absolutely wonderful as the older brother in the original Broadway company of Neil Simon's *Brighton Beach Memoirs*. That was my 19th *Hamlet,* and I'd never seen a production I really thought made me understand what so many other people love in the character of Hamlet. Well, this was the most superb production and the most wonderful performance of *Hamlet* and finally, after all these years, I fell in love with the play in the same way that so many people do the first time they see it, and I understood emotionally what all the screaming was about. A year later I went to an Off-Broadway theater and I noticed Zeljko Ivanek in person in the lobby, and I thought I had to go up and tell him how much I admired his work as an actor, and how much I liked his Hamlet. And so standing in a place where I could observe him, but he didn't see me, I rehearsed what I was going to say, "How do you do Mr. Ivanek. I'd like to tell you how much I admire your work as an actor, ah-ah-ah." I couldn't think of anything to say. I was like 14 years old, totally awkward. I started thinking of things like, "Oh damn, I didn't wear any mascara today!" You know, totally irrelevant things. So I kept trying to go on, "How do you do Mr. Ivanek!" The time to go into the performance came. I noticed where he was sitting, and I thought to myself, "O.K., I'll talk to him in the intermission." I hardly even saw the show, because I was still trying to think of what to say, and thank God, it wasn't something I had to review. There wasn't any intermission, so after the show was over, I got up, I walked out, I noticed him walking out of the theater, and I followed him down the street until he disappeared into the crowd. I could never think of what to say to him, and, of course, I thought it was so idiotic.

I told this to many friends who said, "But, Holly, that's crazy, because you can write at length about his work, but you can't go up and introduce yourself, and say anything to him?" I find it very difficult. I don't find it difficult to interview an actor because I have a job to do, and he or she has a job to do, but just to go up and verbally express my admiration for an artist, then I turn into a 14-year-old-nerd, just shy.

About a year later, I finally realized what was going on. I realized that what I really wanted to say, but I dared not say and couldn't even admit to myself at the time, was, "How do you do Mr. Ivanek! I'd like to tell you how much I admire your work as an actor. Do you go for older women?" I think that's a very funny story on myself.

TO DIFFER FROM THE *TIMES?* HOW COME?

Jonathan Kalb

When I was working for the *Middletown Press,* I wrote an unfavorable review of an Ibsen production at the Yale Rep which *The New York Times* critic liked. The editor of the paper called me into his office the day after the *Times'* review appeared, stared at me for a long moment (to see if he spied guilt, I guess), and said, "Listen! I respect your writing. I think you've been doing a good job, and I don't know anything about the theater. I want you to know that. What I do know, though, is that what *The New York Times* thinks is generally the mainstream opinion—what the average person thinks, or should think, about a theater piece—and your review was just too different from the *Times.*" He actually used the word "different." I listened carefully to him, fascinated by this whole spirit of the conversation, and I remember hoping that someone would interview me some day so I could tell this story. It was such a wonderful snapshot of the status of *The New York* Times' opinion. It was not O.K. with the editor of that provincial paper that his theater critic had an opinion so different from the established norm or mean, and he put it so straightforwardly that I can tell the story years later as a little icon of an important impasse in our culture. What do I think of what the editor said? I think it was cowardly. Did I think so then? I'm not sure. At 21 years I was mostly fascinated that he was bothering to talk to me at all. But the experience had an impact on me. It made me respect my rebelliousness more. It also made me want to write for a place like *The Village Voice.*

REVENGEFUL ARE THE ARTISTS

Walter Kerr

Once I wrote a very unfavorable notice about a very good friend of ours. It's generally true that after such a thing it's sort of risky to get in touch with the artist you've written about, so you plan to lie low for six months. That's what I was going to do, and I was thinking, "Oh God, and now I can't just call him; I can't see him for six months. I'm sorry for that," The telephone rang, and it was he. He talked and he talked about everything else in the world, and I thought, "Isn't he ever going to say anything about the play or the review?" Finally he said, "Walter, listen, I read your notice. I thought there was a certain meretricious truth in it." That was the sting. It was good, because it was balanced: a riddle with a kind of false truth. And yet entirely accurate.

BELIEVE IT OR NOT,
CRITICS CAN APOLOGIZE TOO

Howard Kissel

In 1984 I wrote what I thought an extremely objective, mixed but balanced, review of Stephen Sondheim's musical *Sunday in the Park with George*. I thought it was fair, but it was perceived as negative. About a week later I was at Carnegie Hall and saw a music critic whose judgment I respected. He said, "I thought you were very hard on Sondheim's show."

A few days later was the voting meeting for the annual awards of the New York Drama Critics Circle, and I thought before I voted perhaps I should take another look at *Sunday*.

For the first half hour, I was very angry with myself—and with my friend, the music critic. "I must be crazy to sit through this again," I told my wife. She told me to calm down and take it easy. I said to myself, "As long as you're here, rather than make yourself angry, why not concentrate on the sounds that are coming from the orchestra pit?" I found myself fascinated by the palette of the orchestrations. Little by little the orchestral textures drew me into the show. By the time it was over it had moved me to tears. A day or so later I found a pretext in reviewing a revival of Rodgers and Hammerstein's *Allegro* to retract some—though not all— of what I had written about *Sunday* and to apologize for having been somewhat dismissive of what was obviously a deep and difficult work.

Six months later I ran into my friend—the music critic. "You know what?", he said.

"I eventually came around to your first opinion of *Sunday in the Park with George.*"

A COLD-CUTS-AND-PICKLE FIGHT BETWEEN ARTISTS AND CRITICS

Stewart Klein

One of the most memorable nights in the theater I had was in the '60s. There was a little play at a tiny theater Off-Broadway, downtown in Greenwich Village, about hippies. There were two or three hippies who entered what was supposed to be an abandoned church and spread tablecloths on the floor of the stage, and laid out things for a picnic—cold cuts and potato salad and pickles, and they proceeded to smoke marijuana, and get a little stoned. Then they started throwing these cold cuts at each other and a pickle flew into the audience, and hit a critic named Daphne Kraft right in the forehead. She was a very sweet demure young woman. She blushed and held the pickle, and Edith Oliver leaned over to Daphne and said, "I'll be damned if I let an actor hit me in the forehead with a pickle! Throw it back at him!" Daphne wouldn't. The play went on, and a few minutes later one of the actors picked up a large plate of potato salad and tripped down at the footlights, and this entire plate of potato salad fell into the lap of the formerly blue suit of the critic Emory Lewis, and Edith Oliver leaned over to him and said, "Emory would you like to have a pickle with your potato salad?" I went on the air that night and reported all of the above. I don't think I said a word about the play except that it was a stiff.

LOSE NOT YOUR FAITH IN ART!

Jack Kroll

About ten years ago a new play by Jack Gelber was put on in the American Place theater. I have a great respect for his play *The Connection,* which caused a lot of changes in the American theater, and I got to know him pretty well over all these years. I was invited to a symposium about this new play of his. So I went to the performance; there were all the other critics and the audience, and the playwright and me, and it turned out that I was the only guy there who didn't like the play. Extremely awkward situation! What happened was that the symposium degenerated into a terrible fight between me and Jack. I was trying to be very careful in my criticism, very objective and mild. He began to yell and scream at me right there

Part IV
Memo
For The Critics
From The Theater–Makers

1 MIXED FEELINGS: THEATER-MAKERS COMMENT ON CRITICS AND CRITICISM IN PRINCIPLE

Playwrights/Lyricists, Directors, a Composer, and an Actress:

Glenn Close
Zelda Fichandler
Richard Maltby
Lynne Meadow
Arthur Miller
Gregory Mosher
Harold Prince
Richard Schechner
Peter Shaffer
Stephen Sondheim
Ellen Stewart
Wendy Wasserstein
August Wilson
George Wolfe

Producers:

Emanuel Azenberg
Andrè Bishop
Richard Jay-Alexander
Rocco Landesman
Margo Lion
Arthur Rubin
James Walsh
Robert Whitehead

Press-agents:

Shirley Herz
Fred Nathan

They answer the questions:

- What's your attitude towards theater criticism?

- How has theater criticism changed over the years you've been working in the theater?

- What are the main problems of theater criticism today?

GLENN CLOSE

I don't read critiques of theater productions I'm in because I'm too sensitive and I know that no matter what anyone says—good or bad—I will have to walk out on the stage the next night. Good criticism can make you self-conscious, especially if particular moments in your performance are singled out. And as far as negative criticism is concerned, I try to be coldly objective about my work and the work of those around me so I am usually aware of weakness and flaws—of the attempts to solve problems. I know how hard everyone has worked and who is responsible for the results. A lot of times, critics just get it wrong and it can make for very frustrating reading.

A lot of critics in this country have their own agendas—they don't really come to something with true objectivity. For example, I recently performed on Broadway in a play called *Death and the Maiden.* My co-stars were Richard Dreyfuss and Gene Hackman. All of us are actors who have deep roots in live theater. (I did theater for 10 years before my first movie role). There were some critics who chose to label us as "movie-stars" and who intimated that we didn't belong on stage and were somehow not valid for theater. It was destructive ultimately to the New York theater community because a climate was created that will not encourage actors like us to come back to their roots.

Some critics write to create controversy and sell newspapers. They try to find something sensational or nasty. They love themselves more than they love theater. Their survival is more important to them than the survival of a rich and varied theater tradition. Good criticism doesn't just feed off what it criticizes. It should be constructive, not *de*structive.

There are many actors I know who refuse to work here, not because they are afraid of criticism but because they don't see the need to expose themselves to unfair, biased, vicious, and ignorant criticism. Life is just too short!

ZELDA FICHANDLER

It seems to me that in our country critics are there to sell newspapers and therefore everything has to be in terms of, "Is it good?", "Is it bad?", "Should you go?", "Should you spend your money somewhere else?" Instead of being an attempt to identify it for what it is, they identify it for whether it will sell.

I had good luck with critics. I can't really complain about the level of intelligence, articulateness, and caring of the critics in Washington over the long run. Richard Coe of *The Washington Post,* who was the critic when we had just begun, actually helped to create our institution. He is one of the creators of the Arena Stage because he understood the aim and not only evaluated it point by point (each production being a point), but he evaluated it on a continuum. Most critics review productions like a linear series of potatoes in a supermarket. Richard Coe was able to see the connection between all these.

RICHARD MALTBY

I pay attention to critics for business reasons. From my point of view, a review is an aspect of business. Are your reviews good enough for the show to run? What sentences can be pulled out to make people want to see the show? But I also believe that writers always win, and this is what I keep telling my young playwright friends who get slaughtered by critics. Critics ultimately don't have the power, and it's wrong to give them power over you. One day they like you, the next day they don't like you. It doesn't matter, because if the work is good, the work prevails.

LYNNE MEADOW

Criticism is a necessary thing, like the sun: it comes up every morning and comes down every night. There are critics who teach us sometimes about the work we do and who help us to learn; there are some critics who don't help us to learn.

ARTHUR MILLER

Before, with very few exceptions, the American theater was reviewed by reporters who were simply working on the base of common sense. They had no special education in drama. However, there were a few who were very good. The bulk of criticism was basically reportage. But it was a very democratic theater; it was much more of a mass theater than we have had since World War II. There could be an O'Neill or a few other ambitious playwrights, as well as some European avant-garde. Then—around, I would say, may be the '60s—the academic critics came in. They suspected popular theater while at the same time they wanted to be part of it. It was very ironical. A few of them wanted to be directors, even actors, writers. So the critic came to be in competition with the artist for public recognition. On the whole, it was bad for the theater.

All I ask personally is that critics love the theater. Many of them seem to resent it. But, in general, and I'm not the first one to say this, the critics that are regarded as being most perceptive, most intelligent are the ones who are most negative. The critics that praise—people think, "He's not as clever!"
- **You must have very contradictory feelings towards the critics. In the beginning they have helped you a lot.**
Arthur Miller: Yes!
- **And afterwards the American critics especially haven't been that good to you.**
Arthur Miller: Well, they changed, and I did, too.
- **Would you compare criticism in the United States and in Europe?**
Arthur Miller: It is changing. I would say that the American critic has been less likely to inquire about the thematic structure of a play, he's been far more pragmatic. This could be a good thing, but it could also limit his scope. The European critic long ago took for granted that literature had to do with politics, with everything. Here we have a tradition that they are separate and apart; theater has to do with entertainment, primarily. That has had a good effect and a bad one; the American

play in general is pressed to be very active compared to the average European play, which is more likely to be discursive and philosophical. There's also another element and that is that for a long time, for many of the avant-garde critics and many of the popular critics here, an American play could never be taken quite as seriously as any European play. There's a comical irony in this. They see the world from New York, and New York, of course, is one more province of the world. For example, in the '50s especially and '60s, the idea was that only in Europe, and especially in England, was there a theater of any consequence, but if one went to England at the time, one found that the main inspiration came from the American theater, American acting, and American plays after 1956, 1957...

- **What's your explanation for that?**

Arthur Miller: Ignorance, I suppose. They just didn't now the situation. The American playwrights were being derided here and were among the most important ones in England and elsewhere.

- **You've said that you are a playwright without a reviewer in the corner. What are the advantages and the disadvantages of such a position?**

Arthur Miller: I'm too old to worry about this anymore, but at certain times in life, you want to feel support for what you are trying to do, someone who understands you. The closest I ever came to that was Harold Clurman, but aside from him I had nobody. On the other hand, maybe that makes us tougher than the playwrights in other countries who have more support. In any case, my plays are more frequently produced now, both here and abroad, than at any time in the past.

GREGORY MOSHER

There's some good theater criticism in America, but in New York, at least, most critics forgo the possibility of aesthetic commentary for something quite different, consumer reporting. Critics have become judges, as if shows and artists were so much fruit in a stall. "Yummy Peaches!" "Yucky Grapes!" "Apples Might Be Good But DON'T BUY Until I Let You Know." This is especially true at *The New York Times,* of course, where they have established themselves as the ultimate, in effect only, judge. It is as if there were a fence separating the show and the audience, and the *Times'* critic was the gatekeeper who controlled the access. This sad approach degrades the art, the artists, and the critics themselves. It is a materialistic approach to an adventure of the spirit.

- **But then why do producers go along with it?**

Gregory Mosher: For precisely these materialistic reasons. When a show is ratified by the *Times,* the rewards are immediate and enormous. So the producers tend to kowtow to the press. We quote them in ads and in front of our theaters. We endure their contempt because THEY CAN MAKE US RICH! But this is a dangerous game. For almost twenty years, the box office has risen steadily. But each year it does it on fewer shows with few actors, with no investment in the future in the form of young writers. It is the mega-hits, the theme parks of the industry, and their huge ticket prices which have *created a false sense of health.*

- **Why not just fight the *Times?***

Gregory Mosher: Not pass by the gatekeeper? Go over or around the fence? Well, there are various ways you can do that. But they're not stupid. They see what you are doing, and they resent it. They *like* being the *judge,* and if you don't play by the rules, they have countless ways of getting back at you. They take it very personally if you fight for your show. They deny this, of course, but it is laughably obvious. Finally, there is a feeling that fighting the *Times* "just isn't done." It's considered bad form, immature, "Artistic." And so the writers, actors, designers and craftspeople of the theater are caught in a game that is played between the theater owners, producers, and the *Times.*

I don't think this situation exists in any other art form, or enterprise of any sort, for that matter. Everybody *wants* the support of the *Times,* but even without it politicians get elected, buildings are built, restaurants flourish, movies make millions. Only in the theater do we bow down to the gatekeeper.

I believe that, unless an alternative is found to this madness, we will speak of the theater as we do of vaudeville, as a charming but unfortunate extinct pastime. You don't have to be a genius to see that we've hardly any time until we lose our audiences and our artists for good.

HAROLD PRINCE

I do believe that if there were no critics, fewer people would go to the theater. There's too much to see and too much to do, and contemporary advertising misleads and overwhelms, putting quality theater in jeopardy.

RICHARD SCHECHNER

The structure of American theater criticism is basically wrong . If you read *The New York Times'* Book Review section, they have many, many people reviewing books: novelists, scholars, poets, and the people who review the book of a particular person usually know a great deal about that person's career. For theater, they have three or four people, writing all the reviews. Frank Rich and Mel Gussow have to know everything. The paper should have reviewers or theater critics who are not doing everything. They should have 20, or 30, or 40 people in New York. For example, they should have me for an experimental performance; if it's about Broadway, they might ask Brooks McNamara; if it's about a show from England, they might ask somebody who knows about English drama. But the reason they don't do this is because the main function of the theater criticism in the United States is to sell the play or to stop selling the play. It's a consumer guide; it's not really about what the play is about. They allow the book reviewers to use many, many hundreds of words. In the theater reviews, it's only a few words. The book review comes out only once a week; the theater review—every day. The theater review should be like the book review. It should go out once a week and it should have room for many, many words. It should discuss the plays in depth. They should have two or three reviewers look at each performance from different perspectives. So right now it's not worth much. And *The New York Times* is the best in the whole country. If you go to other newspapers, it's usually people without theater training. It's kind of: if they don't do anything else, they can do theater. It's so ignorant. It's always talking about whether it's good or bad, and it has a few banal cliches; it's tedious. It's not the worth of even good toilet paper.

PETER SHAFFER

What's the point of the critics? It's ridiculous! Why should a playwright be in this position all the time: all his life being a schoolboy and passing an exam every time he writes a play! "What do the critics say? What does the Daily this say? What does the Daily that say?" It's like being a perpetual child, as if you are passing your matriculation every two years: a contemptible situation to be in. You might say to me, "You may learn something from it." I suppose it's possible, but I don't honestly think I've learned very much from critics. Most of them, when they like me, praise me—which is nice; when they don't like me, they abuse me—which I feel keenly and it shakes my confidence. But I don't learn anything much from either position. I learn by going to the theater, watching and experiencing, and working with actors. Also from watching audiences. When I'm particularly hurt by a critic, I remember one thing which offers a little spiteful and inadequate consolation: he exists because of me; I pay his bills—I and my colleagues. Without my writing a play, he wouldn't be in that profession, unless he would confine himself totally to reviewing playwrights who are dead—which, I suspect, is much the position that a lot of critics would like playwrights to be in.

There's a tendency among critics which really annoys me: to put down one's work almost in proportion to the degree to which the public has enjoyed it. It's a kind of snobbery. There's so much rubbish in the world which masses of people like and I detest: so I can't claim that popular enjoyment is the sole criterion of excellence. Nevertheless, in a live art it is highly relevant. On a serious level, I strive to satisfy my audience.

I happen to believe that narrative skill is one of the most important skills in the theater. Nowadays critics tend to look down on it. They say, "Oh, that's merely a storytelling!" Actually storytelling is a very hard thing to do. A lot of modern playwrights simply could not do it to save their lives, and a lot of critics tell them, "That's all right! Narrative is only a small ingredient in theater." Rubbish! It is paramount. Ask Shakespeare! I'm probably regarded by some critics as very simple-minded for saying this, but I don't think I am. It's essential for a playwright to be able to know what the proper shape, force, and end of his story is.

STEPHEN SONDHEIM

I pay no attention to critics. I don't care about them. And the only one that matters is *The New York Times*. As soon as you pay serious attention to a critic, you've dignified him, and I don't do that.

ELLEN STEWART

I respect theater criticism. I don't always agree with critics. When we began, they wouldn't even come to see our shows. I've watched their attitude change and they have begun to see theater in much different light than they used to. They were nuts, not just for me, but for the international theater. When Tadeusz Kantor was here in 1978/79, *The New York Times* gave him a bad review. That was the mentality of the American critic. Tandeusz Kantor is like a God now in this country. Much of our work that critics wouldn't come to see has now become American classics. Now they are knowledgeable, whereas they were not before.

Many critics are frustrated playwrights and directors, and actors, and they don't do any of those things very well, so they become critics and psychologically their opinions are colored by their frustration.

WENDY WASSERSTEIN

Criticism is part of the process. It's interesting, though, when I go and speak places, I'm always asked first about the critics and *The New York Times'* critic. Plays take forever to write and then you have to cast them and to rehearse, and critics come at the end. It's hard; it's scary. I don't think one ever would be able to be immune to it. Because if you are any good, you care about what you did a lot, and as my friend Christopher Durang says, "It's random!" So it can be that someone likes your play, and that's the person who happens to review your play. Or the person who happens to review your play is the person who hates your play.

AUGUST WILSON

I take theater criticism always straight. I read all the reviews about my plays—the good ones and the bad ones. I learn from all of them. For instance, critics will sometimes describe the characters in a way I haven't thought of. They'll say that one character is industrious. Oh, yes, he is industrious! I've learned a lot of things like that. Also, when they tell the story, each of them approaches it differently, and sometimes I'm surprised that it can be told that way. As for the reviews that are not positive, I try to find out how they arrived at, say, this particular claim. I try to imagine myself viewing it as they viewed it. So I've learned something more about what I'm doing by paying attention to criticism.

- **Your attitude puts you in a quite different position than the usual one of the people "from the other side of the barrier."**

August Wilson: It's a learned response, "You are a critic! Get over there!" I go to the O'Neill Center, for instance, and there are fellow playwrights and critics there. No one wants to sit at the critics' table. There's that artificial separation: if you are a critic, you are an enemy! Maybe because I didn't come up in American theater, I don't really feel that way. I never developed that animosity toward critics, even if they don't give me favorable reviews. I take the bad reviews and put them up on my desk, and I use that as a reminder, because when my next play comes up, I don't want this guy saying that he doesn't like it.

GEORGE WOLFE

Perhaps I'm being romantic, but when one reads about American theater in the '30s and '40s, it seems like there was a greater sense of community, and the critics were a part of that community. Today, critics function primarily as arbiters, deciding, in large part, the financial success or failure of a show. Another problem is that there are a significant number of critics, who due to their cross-cultural limitations and lack of sophistication when dealing with non-European aesthetics, become bullies. Rather than admit what they don't know or understand, they become hostile and try to dismiss and disregard the work. I've been rather fortunate in that for every six critics who just don't get my work, one or two of the brightest and the most significant do.

EMANUEL AZENBERG

There is a good quote from a famous play, "Public postures often take the configurations of a private derangement." That position is taken by intellectual critics very often, by ones that are very self-serving and self-satisfied. They are not open to whatever is on the stage. It's all about "how well I write," not about what was on the stage. If critics would go to the theater with a little bit more humility and less preconception. And many do. There are critics that I genuinely like, and those who are public posturing for whom I have less respect.

I teach at Duke University an anti-intellectual course. It's a course on opinion, and how to have an honest one, not one that—since Pinter is important—you say, "Oh, that's interesting!", and you don't know what the hell happened. I give the students plays to read and I rip the covers off, so they don't know what they are. I want them to write one page: Did it move you? Did you laugh? Did you cry? I want every stomach opinion. I don't want any intellectual nonsense. We'll discuss it intellectually later.

If you were a critic, I would do the same thing. Did you like it? Don't tell me how for three to seven hours you are going to write this wonderful essay. When you go to the theater and you like it, you are saying "Wow!" That's what I want to see on the page, "Wow!"—a sound, because that's what the theatrical experience is. We use simple words. When we start talking about symbolism and so on, forget it! Sometimes you have no opinion and you make one up. How about not having an opinion? "I didn't understand the play!" I've never heard that from a critic. And there had to have been one moment in every critic's life, when he's said, "I don't know!" That should be a review. You can read those reviews: when they don't know what happened, they start telling you stories. We've all seen bad productions of Shakespeare; we fell asleep. Why don't you say, "I fell asleep!" Admit that you were bored. It doesn't mean that it's bad. It means that you were bored. It's no sin. It's a sin when you lie. You create this mystique, so other people say, "I'll be stupid if I don't say: "Yes, it was very good!" There were movies years ago by Antonioni. I didn't know what the hell they were about. Everybody told me they were important movies. Who was I to tell them? So I said, "Yes! Very good!"

And you know you are a fraud when you say, "It was very interesting!" and the truth was—you were desperately keeping your eyes open.

ANDRÈ BISHOP

My attitude towards critics is probably like that of most of the people in the theater: you need them and you love them when they love you, and you don't like them when they don't. Critics have helped us and they have helped many artists. I wish certain things about criticism were better; I wish that certain writers were better, I wish some of the ones that are mean were less mean, but I don't see it as something strange. It's just part of being in the theater. I've tried to find a healthy balance: I don't let rave reviews change my thinking about a play any more than I will let terrible reviews.

What is distressing is that in New York, there's really only one newspaper—*The New York Times*—and basically there's only one critic who counts. The chief critic for the *Times* now is a very good critic. People take him to task, but part of that is because he's very powerful. He's intelligent and a good writer as well. Some of the other critics are not as intelligent and don't write as well, and there's a certain level of gossip in criticism in New York now—a lot of the critics are reviewing Frank Rich as much as they are reviewing the play. It's very gossipy here.

RICHARD JAY-ALEXANDER

I can't worry about critics because they have opinions and they are their opinions. That's why they make chocolate and vanilla: taste is a very personal thing. You may like chocolate; you may like vanilla, but both can exist. Critics have their own axe to grind. Are the critics serving the public; are they serving themselves? I have no idea.

ROCCO LANDESMAN

The ideal critics should be well-trained in dramatic literature. They should know Ibsen and Brecht, and Checkov, and Strindberg, and Shakespeare, but generally they don't. They know what plays they've seen. As a class they tend to be undereducated and under-informed. They are basically going with their gut feeling. Some of them are more intelligent and more knowledgeable than others, but as a rule they don't have ideal training for their profession. There's also a lack of knowledgeability about the practical production. Most of them have never been involved in producing a play. You'd like them to educate themselves about the process of the theater. But they are too lazy. It's a very lazy profession without doubt. Their job is going to the theater for two and a half hours and spending another three hours writing a review—it's a five-hour-work week.

Criticism has gotten worse since I started in the theater. Then there were quite a few adversary critics. Now there're very few of them. There's not that kind of so called left-wing sensibility, with a little more anti-establishment feeling. There're not enough different opinions and that's a problem.

- **With your theater education and practice in teaching and criticism, you are a unique exception among the producers. Do you think that it's a good background for a producer to have been a critic beforehand?**

Rocco Landesman: Sure. It helps to know dramatic literature and to have a perspective on the critics in order to be able to make some assessments how the critics are going to review your work, since their reception is very important for commercial success. It helps to develop your own aesthetic sensibility. You are lost if you continually try to figure out what somebody else is going to like. You've got to start with what you are going to like.

MARGO LION

I'm not a Frank Rich basher. He is a very smart critic and an engaging writer. Most of the time I agree with him. Even on shows that he's reviewed that I've produced, I can see his point—it's an intelligent point of view. He's been very significant in paving the way for important new theater artists who aren't necessarily trying to reach the widest audience. He's really trying to improve the quality of American theater. I also have a very positive feeling about his support of the non-traditional casting.

The problem is that there are no other major critics who carry the weight of Frank Rich.

- **You think that New York criticism boils down to Frank Rich?**

Margo Lion: The rest of the critics all get lumped together: there's Frank Rich, and then there's everybody else, and the everybody else doesn't equal him. No other publication has the respect of *The New York Times*. So I don't think it's really his fault; it's the fault of the system where there's one paper that people really take seriously. On the other hand, Frank does not determine the success of the show. He says that if a producer has a show that enough people want to see, and if the producer has enough money to keep the show running and lets people see it, it'll live. In the end, that's true.

I would like to see more critics, more sources of criticism that are respected so that there're more points of view for the theater-going public to read. The problem now is that there isn't quality in criticism. Frank Rich is in my mind the only real quality writer offering criticism in New York.

ARTHUR RUBIN

I don't mind any critic who honestly criticizes the show. That's what he is—a critic. What I don't like is when they go beyond the bounds of criticism, when they criticize things that have nothing to do with that particular show. They say, for example, that this theater had five flops in a row, prior to this show. That has nothing to do with the show that's playing now. The critics may be a little bit more taken with themselves today. They want to write these flowing, flowery sentences that only they can understand. The average person doesn't know what they are writing about. They want to become authors all of a sudden.

JAMES WALSH

With really one newspaper calling the shots, it currently comes down to, "Do you like Frank Rich?" He is an articulate, erudite critic; he cares; he wants the theater to be at its very best. But I don't think he gives an awful lot of opportunity to anything that doesn't meet his standards, and I don't really know what his standards are. I don't know that he's written in a way that's been helpful. On the contrary, he's been very unhelpful. At least for the commercial theater, he's continually dumping on it, so it makes it harder and harder to do a play. A lot of people have pulled away from the theater because they don't want to take the risk of spending two years to write a play and have this one person tell them whether or not they are going to have future as a playwright. So his role as a critic is a difficult one. All of us would rather produce really major work, but if no one is writing it, what can you do? He has to accept the reality he lives in. And he's still looking for something that isn't there; he's not helping make these writers turn it out. It would be nice if we saw a major critic who had a more helpful view, one that was not angry and cynical. Walter Kerr has written good and bad reviews, but he wrote them in a way that wasn't hard to read, and maybe you didn't like his notice, but you got the feeling he was fair. You didn't feel that, if he didn't like something, he was going to demean you in some way.

To be honest, there're only a few critics who really take their positions seriously. Some of these people are from the news and from the weather, and suddenly they are critics. I remember years ago, when there was a new Tennessee Williams' play— not one of his better ones, but he is a major writer in American drama—and this TV reviewer who was before that an early news reporter was assigned the task of being a critic. That kind of showed you how uninterested the media is in the theater.

I don't pay so much attention to critics anymore. I rarely read reviews anymore.

ROBERT WHITEHEAD

I don't think we have any good critics at the moment. We have some intelligent ones. But we don't really have any imaginative critics in New York. Most critics want to be something else—other than critics, and their desire to be noticed is so great that it gets in the way of their professional point of view. There are very few critics, at any time, whose criticism is rooted in a great love for the theater.

SHIRLEY HERZ

Critics are a necessary evil. In the West End, critics more or less keep their own opinion; they say, "It didn't appeal to me, but it might find an audience!" Here a critic says, "This is bad! That's good!" and doesn't use the personalized "I," or "May be you'll like it." The other side of the coin is that, if they praise it, you don't think about the bad side of it, and you are the first one to take ads and to advertise what they've said.

FRED NATHAN

There are a great number of attractions, and people have only a certain amount of money to spend, so they have to be discretionary. There are certain critics that people have come to rely on, subsequently they follow them up and trust them. I find that the situation is a much better one than not, because if you didn't have a body of critics, you'd get an audience going to see shows that were not worth the price of the admission and a lot of angry people, who might never return to the theater again.

2 LOOKING FOR THE REAL THING: THEATER-MAKERS DEFINE THE ROLE OF CRITICISM IN THE THEATER PROCESS

Playwrights/Lyricists, Directors and a Composer:

Zelda Fichandler
Lynne Meadow
Richard Maltby
Arthur Miller
Marsha Norman
Harold Prince
Lloyd Richards
Richard Schechner
Peter Shaffer
Stephen Sondheim
Wendy Wasserstein
August Wilson
George Wolfe

Producers:

Emanuel Azenberg
Andrè Bishop
James Freydberg
Bernard Jacobs
Richard Jay-Alexander
Rocco Landesman
Margo Lion
Arthur Rubin
Gerald Schoenfeld
James Walsh
Robert Whitehead

Press-agents:

Adrian Bryan-Brown
Merle Debuskey
Bill Evens
Shirley Herz

They answer the question:

- What do you think the ideal role of theater criticism should be in the overall theater process? How can it be compared to the situation that exists today in this field?

ZELDA FICHANDLER

The critic helps to form a bridge of communication between the artwork and the receiver of the artwork. The critic can aid the perceiving ability of the audience. The more you know, the more you can appreciate. A true critic helps me as an audience member in my understanding of the rules-of-play from the artist's point of view, of the desired result, and helps me to see, to hear, to understand in the presence of the artwork in a deeper way than I would without the critic.

If I'm considering producing a play that's been done before in England or some other country, I like to read the reviews. I read them for information.

I'm very disappointed when a person whom I respect sees a work that I've been involved in and doesn't see what the intentions of it were, and attributes its faults to the wrong person. It disappoints me or just saddens me, and sometimes I get very angry. I think, "But didn't you know why that happened that way? Why do you say that's the actress' fault? That was a dreadfully written scene! There is nothing more the actress could have done with that!" I say that to myself; I don't say it to the critic.

It's too bad there isn't a dialogue between the artists and the critic. In this country it's taboo: you don't call up and say, "You know, I think you are perfectly wrong about that. Let me tell you why!" You are supposed to keep a distance as if you two are in different endeavors. A critic should be entering into a dialogue in order to help.

Within the theater you use various people as critics. I consider myself to have been a very good critic at Arena Stage, because I helped the other artists realize their intentions in the work. If you can't be an in-house critic, then you have to be organ-critic—a critic of a certain journal—and at least you should try to know as much as possible about the process.

LYNNE MEADOW

The ideal role of the critic is to inform the public, to keep the sense of standards. One of the goals of critics should be to be aware of the body of work of the artists and not just look at one thing at a time, to understand where something fits in the scheme of things. Sometimes it's missing and only a specific work is looked at and a judgement is passed—Yes or No. It's very important to understand why a director, an actor, a writer is doing something at a particular instant.

Probably most people are critics because they love the theater, and sometimes they are disappointed when it fails, so they become very angry because they have a love. It would be nice if they thought they should communicate that love to the public, because not everybody loves the theater the way critics and people who work in the theater do, and sometimes the public has to be made aware of how wonderful it is.

RICHARD MALTBY

There are two things critics should do. The first is to report to a readership what kind of experience a given show promises, which involves both an assessment of its value and its impact, and an acknowledgment of the emotional and non-cerebral elements of the play.

Frank Rich is a great critic. He is limited in only one quality, which is an ability to respond from the heart as well as from the head. There are shows, particularly musicals, which are indefensible, but you love them. I can recall a particular show- *The Tap Dance Kid*—a conventional show, but with a very attractive story with some wonderful music. He responded only to the conventional aspects of the show, negatively, and didn't acknowledge that if you went to the theater you would be moved, or if you liked this sort of thing you would have a good time. In his review of my show *Baby,* which was largely favorable, he referred to something as having "a touching effect." But he didn't say, "I cried." It would have helped if he had said to his readership, "I was moved, I think you will be too." He also said privately that since his wife had just had a baby, he thought his emotional response was too personal to trust. Well, we were writing that show for people who knew the emotions of having babies. If you limit these emotions by choice, then you are not responding fully to the show.

Theater is indefensible. After all, it's hardly a grown up profession to put on make-up and tell a made-up story in front of a bunch of other grown ups. The strange thing is that we still do it. It's not only an intellectual event. I'd say that the greatest critic that I've every encountered was Kenneth Tynan. What made him great was that he was extremely cerebral and, at the same time, was able to find something soaring in the theatrical experience. Beyond what his mind saw, his heart also responded to the show. He was also capable of going to an absolutely awful play, and writing a very sensitive piece about what it must be like to be an actor who can't pick his job, who must take what work comes along. He was that compassionate and loving. It's as hard to be a good critic as it is to be a... I was going to say: as to be a good playwright, but that's not true. It's terribly, terribly hard to write a play, and it's not hard at all to write a piece of criticism.

- So, as hard as what?

Richard Maltby: The hard part and the reason we don't see a lot of good sensitive criticism is that if you are sensitive enough to respond to all the elements of a play, you probably are good enough to be writing something else and you wouldn't be writing criticism.

ARTHUR MILLER

Critics should encourage the artist as much as possible because, first of all, except in extreme cases, no critic can tell me that a work doesn't deserve to live. Now, there are some works that are so bad that you don't need a critic to tell you that they are going to disappear. The critic should love the potential of the theater— what it could be. He should be a positive force. He should be led by positive feelings, not primarily by destructive force. See, George Bernard Shaw could be extremely negative and mocking, but he always knew instinctively that his job was to enhance and encourage what was possibly good or artists who might become good later.

- **You have encountered such a critic. John Anderson has found in your work something even you haven't realized at the time.**
Arthur Miller: Yes. He saw it, and he was the only one at the time. That would be the job of the critic. And he never said, "That play was a masterpiece." He said, "The play has a real tragic sense in it and you should work on it." That was perceptive. The other ones simply didn't understand the whole thing at all.

MARSHA NORMAN

What passes for theater criticism in America now is more a kind of consumer journalism, as though a piece of theater were a product, which is to be judged faulty or serviceable. In that language only rarely is a product described as "a good buy." And that's very much the language that they use. It's as though the audience has to be warned not to spend their money on pieces of theater. That's how most critics see their job. And that has had a disastrous effect on American theater.

As playwrights, we need to write our bad plays, our plays that don't work, in order to later write the plays that do work. That means that all our efforts need to be seen as part of a long process. We are in a process of creating a body of work; we are not trying to create single wonderful units of work. It's not like we are building automobiles, and we want to build one great automobile after the next. Critics fail to take that process into account; they tend to judge each play separately and either dismiss it or give it a stamp of approval, or simply a check mark of a pass, "That's O.K."

Then, critics seem to have lost their ability to champion writers, which was the thing that the old critics did have. Walter Kerr, for example, was almost completely responsible for creating David Mamet, for saying, "Believe in this guy! Go see his play! Watch what he's going to do next! Look at this talent that's growing in this man." That's the kind of attitude that critics should have. They really have a very violent response to the work and they have driven a lot of people away from the theater. There's one particular critic in Los Angeles who was personally responsible for my stopping to write for almost five years. The review was so vitriolic, so vicious. It was a personal attack. It basically said, "How can you keep writing? This is ridiculous. We don't want to hear from you any more!" That kind of thing. Anyway, that's the disastrous wrong turn that American theater criticism has taken.

Another thing about critics is that they don't know how shows are made, they are unable to tell who did what. Quite often the director will get the praise for something that the writer did; the actors will get the blame for something that the director did. Generally, in a new play, the writer takes the blame for almost everything, when, in fact, the writer may be the author of the play, but the director is the author of the production.

- **How do you see the future of criticism?**
Marsha Norman: We need more women writing criticism for major media. Women as a group are better able to perceive the activities of a group; they are better able

---

The Man Who Had All The Luck

to look and figure out who did what. They don't tend to see theater as an act of a single will which is what male tend to look for. Male will find out who the leader was and blame him or her almost as if it were a war and they were blaming the generals.

Also, I'd like to see more theater writers doing criticism. I'd like to see Wendy Wasserstein, for example, take a year off and take the position at *The New York Times*. That would be thrilling.

On the morning that a play opens, I'd like to see three reviews. That's the main thing that needs to happen. As we no longer have so many newspapers, we need to have lots of voices represented in one newspaper. We've all become very wary about faulty products. The audience has become lazy; they've also fallen into this business of consumer journalism; they have allowed someone to make up their minds for them. People stay at home and they think, "I don't have time and money to waste, so I'll let Frank Rich make my decisions." If you opened the paper, and there were three reviews of something, then you would be forced to be responsible. You'd read them all, or you'd read one and you'd know you hadn't read the others. You would at least be presented with the fact that what these people were saying was simply an opinion.

HAROLD PRINCE

Critics would be as they had been occasionally: theater historians, capable of putting art in a context historically, perhaps even offering useful criticism. Newsmakers are not interested in that; they are interested in selling papers. The sole function of the critic today is to sell tickets. Rarely am I interested in what they have to say. When we brought *The Phantom of the Opera* from Europe, it didn't matter what they had to say. That has only happened twice in my life. I produced *Fiddler on the Roof* in 1964, and at the opening party I was asked whether I would like to hear Walter Kerr's review. "No!," I said, "It doesn't matter!" It wasn't a good review and it didn't matter.

- Do you think that there is a correlation between the level of theater criticism and the level of the theater it criticizes?

Harold Prince: Too much theater criticism in our country is agenda influenced. Let me explain. There is a school of criticism that believes that if something is presented not-for-profit, it must be better;if the artist is hungry, he must be a great artist; if something is presented on a stage the size of a desk, it must be superior to a full-scale production. Well, that doesn't follow, and it has resulted recently in work of inferior quality. I believe we have been infiltrated by weak material, uninformed by artists who have taken the time to learn their craft. We have a considerable not-for-profit life in this country. How many great playwrights has it introduced, how many directors? Too few.

LLOYD RICHARDS

Good criticism is a means toward a greater and more developed understanding of the art. To see, to appreciate, to evaluate and to project—that would seem to me to be a role for a critic. It's very sad that there are reviewers who announce that their role is merely and simply to tell their readers whether or not they liked the play, to save them the trouble of having to spend the money to see it. That's taking responsibility not to the art, but only to a group of people who buy newspapers.

- **Do you think about theater criticism in terms of being destructive and constructive?**

Lloyd Richards: I think of constructive and destructive criticism in terms of development: you are dealing with developing artists and developing art—to be part of that, one can either be destructive or constructive. When a critic looks at a finished piece of work, he/she should be able to say where it fits into the whole spectrum of the art; what works about that artist's intent, and what doesn't. Sometimes a particular effort seems to fall flat on its face. But we shouldn't make a negative thing of failure. Failure is one step before growth, it's a part of growth. What it means is that this particular effort at this particular time didn't work for these and these reasons. This was what seemed to be attempted, and this is where it failed. The effort may have been a noble and ambitious one. It may have been well conceived but not well articulated. A true critic can give an artist that kind of an evaluation and that helps to advance the art, the artist.

RICHARD SCHECHNER

The task of theater criticism is to explore what the particular production in question might be intending and to evaluate whether or not it achieves its own intentions. It should speak mostly to the people making the production and secondarily to the spectators, but it should not evaluate the production unless it wants to discuss the underlying ideology and theory that generates those evaluations. Which is hardly ever done. It just says: such and such performance is magnificent or is terrible and then it says why: because he shouted his lines, or because he stumbled, but it never investigates why shouting lines is bad, or why stumbling is wrong. In other words, it usually is blind to its own ideology, theory. That's why I don't like it. I don't like things that mystify, and theater criticism mystifies on behalf of the dominant aesthetics.

PETER SHAFFER

Dramatic critics rarely help playwrights. In colleges they mainly aid young students to condescend to art. Young people in universities are so filled with critical terminology and standards that have been given to them by academics, they don't seem to have many instinctive feelings about anything anymore. There are some lunatic critics in this country who actually believe their work is more important than that of the creator. They seem to imply that the artist or the writer exists for them—to supply them with material on which their superior work will be done. That's disgraceful, ridiculous, and infuriating!

STEPHEN SONDHEIM

Criticism has only really had an effect on theater in the last 125 years. Almost up to the end of the 19th century it didn't matter what George Bernard Shaw said. People went to Ibsen or not. Theater criticism didn't affect the box-office because theater was the only game in town. The reason theater criticism has its own power now is because there are so many forms of entertainment and the public has so many dollars to spend. When I was president of the Dramatist Guild, everybody said, "We want to have a meeting and go to *The New York Times* and complain. We don't think there should be criticism." I said, "All right! How many people at this table—25 playwrights—would like to have an opening night and no criticism afterwards whatsoever?" Dead silence, because it's the only form of publicity. It's about spreading publicity. That's all it is.

WENDY WASSERSTEIN

What you want ultimately from criticism is: a play to be able to live long enough in order to have an audience.
- **So you see the role of the critics in drawing audience to the theater?**
Wendy Wasserstein: I think so. I'm always a little bit envious of England because they have all these newspapers and all these critics, and people are interested in a playwright's work.

I had a play *Isn't it Romantic?* that was done Off-Broadway and didn't do well the first time. Then I rewrote it. I did go back and read all the reviews because I thought, "If there's something that all of these people have in common, then there's something wrong with the play." In this way criticism is valuable. Actually a critic helped me when this play was first done. It got a not very good review from Walter Kerr. He said that I should be a novelist, not a playwright, and I thought, "This has to do with the action in the scenes and how the scene is staged, and that it isn't propelling itself forward." That helped me to rewrite it.

AUGUST WILSON

The role of a critic in any endeavor is to enhance the art by pointing directions. Critics have this informed opinion and they offer insights, and they can actually move the theater in a certain direction. They can't do very much about the particular play they are watching in that particular night because it's already done, but criticism can guide playwrights; criticism can inspire them for future plays. Ideally that would be the role of a critic. But I want to separate that from the overnight reviewing. And the real situation is that most of what passes for criticism is reviewing. Some of the reviewers may be qualified to communicate to the public what they thought of the particular show, but some of them are not qualified—they have no credentials. Some of them don't know very well the history of the theater or what's going on exactly. One of the phenomena in the American theater is the TV critic. People will watch the news and they'll watch a guy trying to tell you what this play is about and give you his idea in 60 seconds. That passes for criticism. Is it? No! But

they are very influential.
- A lot of people say that critics should be supportive in order to keep the theater alive. Do you agree with that?
August Wilson: No. You are never going to get good work unless the critics do their job. If you support mediocre work, then that's what you'll have; that's what you'll get for the next 10 years. For instance, since I'm a black playwright, black critics feel, "I don't care if he's good or he's bad, I'm going to give him a good review!" That doesn't serve anyone. You can read in the black newspaper about every black play I've ever seen, "It's the greatest thing in the world!" That's not going to help the playwright. Someone needs to say, "You didn't develop your characters. Go back and try again!" Unless you have done that, that playwright will never grow as a playwright, because he thinks he's already where he wants to go. That's a result of supporting mediocre work. It lowers the common denominator!

GEORGE WOLFE

In theory a critic should be a part of the journey of discovery. A writer writes a play. The work is then exposed to a series of people—a director, designers, actors, whose various reflections can and should aid in the evolution of the work. The critic should be just one more reflection. Unfortunately, in today's climate the critic stands at the end of the journey and passes judgement on how everyone else did.

EMANUEL AZENBERG

The critic has to be helpful. He has to be productive. I've had great experiences with critics on a number of plays out of town and it used to be this way: the critic would review the play and you'd ask him, "Tell me what you saw that perhaps we can fix, so I and the playwright can improve the play if it's possible." Plays are living things; they change. Performances, also. Then I don't think the critic has further influence on artistic value. What he has is a readership that he's responsible to. And he should have a broad spectrum. Brooks Atkinson, for instance, saw the musical *Bye, Bye Birdie*, which he didn't like, but he knew the audience did, and he acknowledged that. The British do it better than we do. Every sex farce that runs for 10 years is reviewed by the same critics that review *King Lear* and *Hamlet,* and they put it into the genre. And it's perfectly all right for people who are not intellectuals to go to the theater to see things that suit them. But we have an elitist theater: This is acceptable!; This is not acceptable! There was a British farce that was done here—the audience was hysterical; they were not a normal theater-going audience, but they were on the floor laughing. That audience should be allowed into the theater. Maybe after they see things like that farce, they could see something else, and going to the theater can become part of their lives. So, there's an audience, there is a productivity, there is an honesty that is necessary—the critic's got to balance all these things. And maybe the most important thing for him to say is, "In my opinion," rather than dictate everybody else's opinion.

The critic should also have some human understanding of the theater process. There are a lot of people who get together to do a play. Whether they are right or wrong, they think that what they are doing is the greatest thing that ever happened. Their souls are on the line. They cannot and should not be ridiculed. It's unfair and it's cowardly, because you have no antagonist. Tell that to me! You'll say something in the way John Simon or Frank Rich write on occasion; I'll hit you and you won't have teeth. But in the paper you can hide behind freedom of speech. On the streets that I come from, you don't talk like that. So it's a little humanity that's required. You don't have to like it, but you have to recognize that there are people who do like it. I'll do everything I can to exist with or without you.

ANDRÈ BISHOP

The ideal for criticism includes: an open-mind, an ability to understand the world of the play and the production, an ability to write well, to criticize, but from a positive point of view. Most of us in the theater can take negative criticism. There are often plays I've produced that I don't think have been so good! I understand that. How can one not? What I don't like, what is harmful for artists, is not a bad review but a nasty review. One must say; "I don't think that this play works for this and this reason." There's no reason to be mean.

Reviews for most artists are practicalities. They simply mean that the play is going to run or not. I don't know many artists who read reviews and say, "Aha, he or she is right about my work, and I see now that I've made a mistake, and I must change."

JAMES FREYDBERG

When you are out of town, criticism can help you as a producer to decide whether what you think you are seeing other people are seeing also. For instance, if you think there's an emotional scene, and if a critic comes in and suddenly doesn't see that as an emotional scene, then obviously you are not presenting it in the way you should. Once we got nine bad reviews. Everyone of the reviewers said that the new script was not working. So we went back to the original script and came into New York and got quite good reviews.

But when you are in New York, everything has already been done and it's such a different type of business here—it's either you are accepted or you aren't. Here criticism is just a chance to use the reviews as an advertising vehicle.

BERNARD JACOBS

I don't know if there's an ideal solution. Obviously, from the point of view of the entrepreneurs, they would love critics who are in love with everything. But if that happens, the public would have no respect for them. You can't expect the critics to say that bad things are good. I don't expect that.

They do not have to be as harsh as they are, they do not have to apply an unrealistically difficult standards. Remember that just because they don't like something, it doesn't mean it's bad. Many times the critics have been proven wrong by the audiences. But in this economic climate, with the very high cost of running a show, it's very difficult to fight after you get bad reviews. I'd hope the criticism was different, but again, I don't want to see bad plays or bad productions get good reviews. That doesn't help the theater. The only difference is that things that very often the critics think are bad I think are good, so I'd like to see those productions get better reviews, and obviously I'm not in the position to write the reviews.

Years ago I was in Sardi's restaurant, and the man who was the managing editor of *The New York Times* passed by my table and sat down, and said to me, "You don't like that critic, do you?" I said, "No, I don't think he's a very good critic." He said, "Who would you like to be the critic of the *Times?*" I said, "You would be very wise if you chose me as your critic." He said to me, "You mean you would give up your job to be the critic of the *Times.*" I said, "No, what I'd like to do is to have my job and be the critic of the *Times.*" He, of course, laughed. I don't think I'd like to be a critic because you have to have a kind of a malevolent streak in you. There's a certain amount of meanness that's required. Critics are not constructive, they are essentially destructive. When you read all the reviews, you'll see that there's a certain nastiness in most of them. They love to be sarcastic, humorous at the expense of the creative people.

RICHARD JAY-ALEXANDER

I still believe word-of-mouth is the best critic because *Les Miserables* got terrible reviews when it opened in London, but the people loved it and stood and cheered it. *The Phantom of the Opera* got terrible reviews in New York. It's one of the biggest successes of all time. Where does that put the critic? The critic seems to be necessary when people aren't familiar with the piece. The critics couldn't make or break our shows because the shows were bigger than them.
- **You are lucky to be among "the chosen."**
Richard Jay-Alexander: That doesn't make it feel any better, because you would like the critics' approval. There's nothing like the job of working really hard and then reading a great review. *Les Miz* has gotten consistently wonderful reviews since we opened in New York. So I'm very proud. To read someone who understands the fabric of a show like this, which is so spiritual and so satisfying to work on, can make you cry.

The critic has the responsibility to his reading public—to put an opinion out there. But I do believe that some critics don't write critiques, they get involved in the politics of a show. They never evaluate the design, for example, and they never analyze the piece. They talk about everything else. They turn into gossip columnists.

ROCCO LANDESMAN

Intelligent criticism is always useful. A lot of people who are really angry that the critic doesn't like their show consider the criticism destructive. I don't think that's fair. I've had many negative reviews but because they've been intelligent, they've been helpful to the shows. I hired a critic who wrote one of them—Jack Viertel. I remembered his review and, when I came to Jujamcyn Theaters, the first thing I did was I said to him, "Come, work for me!" Now, his my creative director.

MARGO LION

Some people feel that a critic should report what he sees that night—that includes the audience' response and what's going on in the theater—and not try and have an agenda other than that. They feel that critics shouldn't have a kind of personal vision of the theater which, I think, is what Frank Rich is often criticized for. I don't actually agree with that. I don't mind Frank's point of view. I don't mind if he's said, "I'm going to shape the future of the contemporary American theater." That's sort of interesting. It's courageous. What I don't like is when critics get nasty in a gratuitous way and make readers feel like they are sour on the theater; this makes people not excited about going to the theater. Critics should have a love for the medium. I'd like to see them write with that kind of joy. If they are disappointed, they certainly should say it. That's their job. But commercial theater is a business that's struggling to stay alive, and theater is a very important art form. Criticism should reflect a passion for the medium—that's what we all need.

ARTHUR RUBIN

There should be rotating critics. I don't think one critic should be the main one. Each paper should have a team of critics, so that we don't have to fear Frank Rich. The more people speak about the theater and have their opinions, the better off the theater is going to be. It doesn't have to be such a big job. We put too much stock on *The New York Times'* critics and it just could be very harmful to the theater.

GERALD SCHOENFELD

Ideally, criticism should be constructive. What do I mean by constructive? Every art-form needs to be nurtured and encouraged, and the theater is a very fragile art-form. It doesn't receive government subsidies, and it pays taxes. I'm talking about the Broadway theater. And everybody that I know, that works in the theater, seeks to do the best possible work that they can. Nobody seeks to do what we call a grade B movie. We are not doing *Terminator 2* or something of that nature—although some people may say some of our musicals are like that. But the nature of the art-form and the business is such that most of the things fail. So they should be criticized but not condemned and ruined, and made to look foolish. Theater is a fragile environment, and it should be treated with respect. Criticism should seek to improve, to encourage, rather than to destroy.

The reality is: we happen to be living in a period of negative journalism, also in a period when a large number of people who are engaged in electronic media are performers rather than critics, or in addition to being critics. The journalists who're writing criticism should remember that their criticism is not timeless. Most works that received praise in the past are totally irrelevant today, and the people who praised them in those days, if they had the ability to look into the future, would probably have modified their reviews somewhat. So critics are not writing for posterity and should have more tolerance of their own limitations. They also pride themselves on not taking into consideration what they think the public reaction would be and only convey their own personal standards. That is very good, providing the audience—their readership—knows exactly what those personal standards are: who are these people?; what is their background, their education?; are they single?; are they married?; what is their religion? So that people could be able to take into consideration the criticisms from the source.

Critics are totally intolerant of any standards of perfection other than the ones that they themselves impose. And since there's no objective criteria, and they all come to it from different vantage points, the public is not able to really decide the differences between them. And since they also write for different publications, the power of their respective source should be taken into consideration as well, because even though they may not be as competent as somebody else, the organ that they are writing for, or speaking for, has an importance. If they take all of those factors into consideration, then they could write something which is constructive and helpful, rather than something that is devastating and damaging not only to the work itself, but to the people who are involved with it. There was a critic in Boston—Elliot Norton—he always found a way to be helpful. I think that if more critics were like him, the theater would be much better off, it would be a lot more hospitable place for people who want to work in it.

We live in a society where, if you are not 10, you are imperfect, and the public has been conditioned to accept and want perfection, especially when they are paying high prices. And when somebody says, "It's a 9," that right away shows that 10 per cent is imperfect, and you don't wish to support imperfection with your money or your time. It's very difficult for all components of a show—every actor, the scenery, the design, the costumes, the direction—to achieve a standard of perfection. Today the conclusion really should be: does this play move you, entertain you, or whatever; not: is each individual element of it perfect? If you use that standard almost nothing will stand up.

JAMES WALSH

Because I'm in the commercial theater, I can't separate myself from that. I would like to think that criticism gave the audience an idea what it was the critic saw, without a judgement of it. When I say judgement, I mean you should write a piece objectively, but we all know that every audience is different. Good criticism should help to improve the art. It should aim at its highest possible standards, but also be reflective of the culture within which we all live. We all would like to see Shakespeare and O'Neill, and all of the great playwrights be born every day, but you live with what you have. Maybe the best writers that ever lived aren't writing right now, but the ones that are writing shouldn't be dismissed and discouraged. That intimidates them, and it's not healthy. We need criticism that allows writers to be able to write and fail, not destroying them, so that they could get up again and do it all over. By the time a play gets to Broadway or even Off-Broadway, so much effort has gone into getting it there, so you'd like to think that somebody's going to give you a little bit of credit just for trying it.

ROBERT WHITEHEAD

The ideal role of criticism is that the critic possesses wit and is able to see the theater in relationship to society. A critic who truly cares about the theater's relationship to the world we live in will probably be an interesting critic.
- **Have you met such a critic?**
Robert Whitehead: There was some of that quality in Brooks Atkinson. He wasn't as penetrating a critic as Walter Kerr but he was a great citizen and he deeply cared about the theater. Over a period of 35 years of criticism, what he was as a human being emerged through his work. There was a strong sense of responsibility in the whole of his work.

ADRIAN BRYAN-BROWN

We all hope that a critic will be an honest journalist, reporting on what he sees at the theater. We have unrealistic expectations about them as people—we expect them to be superhuman. If they've had a lousy day or don't feel well, we presume they can put that aside and report without prejudice. We ask that they consider the audience's reaction, and, even if they don't like the show, we want them to be able to say, "It wasn't to my taste, but the people around me were having a great time." We would like all critics to say in their review if they've walked out early. We apply standards to critics we don't apply to ourselves.

Beyond this, producers want to use the critics to help them sell the show. They need favorable quotes which use strong, active language. Business thrives on copy like, "Run, do not walk, to the box office to buy a ticket." This has little to do with critical analysis and gives a lot of importance to what critics say. We exploit what the critics say when it's positive and berate them when their comments are not favorable!

Producers also have a hard time understanding that critics are not part of the theater industry. Their first responsibility is their newspaper or magazine. As much as we would like them to support the theater by writing enthusiastically about plays, it is unreasonable to expect them to be supportive of work they don't like. I do think that critics should have some experience working on a production at some point in their career, to try to fully understand the process of making a play happen. Many critics have lost touch with the human endeavor required to produce a play.

In New York now, the daily critics have too much time—and often too much space to write reviews. The excitement of a spontaneous gut reaction to a production has been replaced by a more informed lengthy essay which may give too much attention to something that really doesn't warrant it.

Television criticism is very important. You are reaching out to a huge audience which doesn't traditionally go to the theater. It makes a large potential market think about live performance as an entertainment alternative.

- Do you think that there is a correlation between the level of theater criticism and the level of the theater it criticizes?

Adrian Bryan-Brown: Most of the critics are very intelligent people and they are frustrated by most of what they see, which is not of a very high intellectual standard. Critics usually come from a literary background that popular theater quite often doesn't have. In many ways most critics are overqualified.

MERLE DEBUSKEY

In the best sense of it, criticism can be important and helpful if the critic is able to communicate his thoughts in a concise, interesting, entertaining, and informative fashion. In order to be a knowledgeable critic, one must know a lot about what makes theater. One has to learn that. You can't become knowledgeable about the craft of the theater by being a designated critic by the media. You may be a very good journalist, a very good writer, an intellectual, but that doesn't mean you are a good critic. You have to know what the essentials are. I don't think that we have the ideal circumstances and we certainly don't have the ideal critics, but it may not be because these people are not capable.

BILL EVANS

The ideal role of criticism is to be a communicator of enthusiasms and dissappointments in an engaging way which leaves room for the reader to have thoughts of his own. At the base of theater criticism, one assumes, is love of theater.

- What are you ideas in regard to defining criticism as destructive and constructive?

Bill Evens: Some critics are very happy and stimulated in their chosen profession. Others seem to be frustrated, disgruntled writers who never intended to be critics and resent the fact that they are. Some sit there watching a play, silently convinced that they could have done better. They envy the playwright (and in some cases his money). These feelings can lead to destructive reviews (and ulcers).

SHIRLEY HERZ

Criticism is to say what's up on the stage. They have to say whether it's good or bad. But it's so subjective. Perhaps there should be two critics from *The New York Times* on the same night and appear in the paper the same day.

3   FINGER IN THE WOUND: THEATER-MAKERS ON CRITICS' POWER

Playwrights/Lyricists and Directors:

Zelda Fichandler
Richard Maltby
Harold Prince
Lloyd Richards
Peter Shaffer
August Wilson

Producers:

Emanuel Azenberg
James Freydberg
Rocco Landesman
Robert Whitehead

Press-agent:

Merle Debuskey

They answer the question:

- What do you think about the power of the critics? Should it be diminished?

ZELDA FICHANDLER

To diminish the critics' power—that would be nice. But how will we do that? I can't imagine a critic not having the role of an advertiser in America. The only way to diminish their power is for the theater to have a direct dialogue with its audience.

RICHARD MALTBY

I don't believe that critics have ultimate power. They have power over making your individual commercial production run, but if your work has distinction, that distinction will prevail and the work will live.

I had a show called *How Do You Do? I Love You!* The first review I got out of town had as its headline, *"Goodbye! I hate you!"*, and it went on to say that we

145

were talentless and we should never show our faces in the theater again. I thought, well, that's kind of good, because once the press has said, "Get out of town!" and you get up, and go to the typewriter the next day, they can never touch you, because what worse can they do? Sure, if the press gangs up on you, they can kill a production, and it can hurt a lot. But I can't imagine a show that has real merit that won't find enough supporters to give it a future life. Maybe it's just that I've been lucky, because my shows have had future lives, regardless of the responses of the critics.

HAROLD PRINCE

I don't think you can diminish the power of the critics. It would have been nice if *The New York Times* had put on a second daily critic. But it seems to me the *Times* is conflicted. It protests that it doesn't want to turn thumbs up or down on a production. Yet when its critic likes a show that few others have liked, it schedules interviews and promotes the show—often to hit status. When it's time for the annual Tony awards, the *Times* places special features on the people it would like to win those awards. Is that because its heart is in the right place? Possibly. But it's also possible that it doesn't want to be wrong, that it wants to define what succeeds and what fails.

- It's usually said, that the producers are to be blamed for giving power to the critics.

Harold Prince: Don't blame producers. What's to be blamed is the absence of newspapers.

LLOYD RICHARDS

To diminish the power of the critics, one need only to have more of them. You could listen to different voices and among them find the persons who you feel most often apply your values and represent your point of view. A critic should say, "I have a particular point of view; other critics have another one. Check us all out and then go make up your own mind." This is what criticism could say. Instead they say, "I don't like it, so forget it!"

I certainly don't and wouldn't want critics to lower their standards, or not to criticize in terms of their knowledge, but there is joy that some of them seem to get from being able to say quotably nasty things about artists. There are critics who, by virtue of the power of their particular publication, have become stars in their own right—greater stars than these whom they may deign to review. That's unfortunate.

PETER SHAFFER

Critics have power in a country like America because the average New Yorker doesn't want to go to the theater very much; he wants every excuse not to go. This city, which is meant to be democratic and remarkably bold in its differences of opinion, is actually highly conformist. *The New York Times* says, "Go!"—we go; *The New York Times* says, "Don't go!"—we don't go. It's grotesque! It's always been grotesque ever since I came here. The critic—whether Atkinson, Taubman, Kauffmann, or Barnes—drew his power entirely from being in this specific position on the *Times*. It's ridiculous and to me incomprehensible.

AUGUST WILS0N

There's one particular critic who occupies what everyone considers a very powerful voice in the theater. He supposedly has the power to close the show if he doesn't like it. Well, I think that's a mythological power! My memory may be faulty, but I have not personally seen, since I've been in the theater, any particular play that this critic gave a bad review and the play closed. There have been some plays that have closed, but you go back and look at the reviews: they got 12 bad reviews by all the critics across the board. I can personally say that if there's this power to close the show, it doesn't work in reverse. Which is why I dispute the power. I personally have gotten great reviews from this particular critic, but I had my show closed two months later. So I say: this man goes and he sees the show, and he writes what he thinks, and it's largely mythological power. What I have seen is that he has encouraged some shows in nonprofit theaters to move into the commercial arena. And here again, that's only an opportunity. It doesn't guarantee that people want to come and see it.

EMANUEL AZENBERG

I don't believe the critics have as much impact as we like to pretend. Most of the time the public makes up its mind—if you can run long enough so the public *can* make up its mind—five or six weeks.
- **But then why do so many people complain about the critics' power?**
Emanuel Azenberg: Because they have to blame somebody. As things diminish, you have to point the finger. So we'll point the finger at the management; the management will point the finger at the critic, and the critic will point the finger back here, and we'll point at the actors who are not here.

We've made a big mistake making *The New York Times* important. It doesn't affect Neil Simon and the musicals, but plays without stars are very vulnerable to the *Times*. Do I think that's why we have so few plays? Obviously not. It's because the playwrights aren't writing them; the actors don't want to act in them, and the economics is terrible.

JAMES FREYDBERG

I don't think critics have the power that the most people think. We give them the power. We put so much emphasis on them. If we financed our shows correctly, we wouldn't have to do that. The hatred of *The New York Times* is created by the fact that the producers become dependent on the paper. There's an attitude that if you don't have a good review you are closing. My attitude is: you wouldn't close a restaurant if the *Times* doesn't like it, so why would you do that with a theater piece?

ROCCO LANDESMAN

It's unfortunate that only one critic has a big economic impact—the critic of *The New York Times*. He is a very able critic, but you wouldn't want to see that much power concentrated in one person. That's dangerous. It would be much healthier if we had a situation like in London, where there are many newspapers.

ROBERT WHITEHEAD

The power of the critics here is kind of a terrible accident. The newspapers all disappeared, so you finally have one newspaper left that means anything to the theater, and that's a misfortune. But we just have to cope and live with it. It is also a big misfortune for *The New York Times*.

MERLE DEBUSKEY

The power of the critics, like the power of anybody in excess, is evil and destructive. There is a very prominent critic who, when attacked, responded by saying that he didn't close the play—the producer did. That's sophistry, because why would the producer close it, if it could exist. You can't run it if there aren't people coming to see it, and one of the reasons they are not coming to see it is that a negative review doesn't allow it to live long enough for people to determine for themselves whether they wish to go see it.

4   A PART OR APART? (THEATER-MAKERS ON CRITICS' NEUTRALITY)

Playwrights and Directors:

Zelda Fichandler
Marsha Norman
Harold Prince
Peter Shaffer
August Wilson

Producers:

Emanuel Azenberg
Andrè Bishop

They answer the questions:

- **Do you think critics should refrain from being friends with theater people?**

- **Do you think critics are/should be a part of the theater community?**

- **Do you think critics should attend rehearsals?**

ZELDA FICHANDLER

If critics went to rehearsals, it would give them the curse of too much information. They will be called subjective and this would take away their ability to judge it, so called, objectively, as if criticism could be objective! First of all, it's impossible, and second of all, objectivity is not even desirable. It's arrogant to think that you can stand outside the work and still define it.

MARSHA NORMAN

They've kept themselves very much apart and they know almost nothing about what they are seeing. They should be a part of the theater community. Absolutely! If they don't know any more than the ordinary theater-goer, then the review might as well be written by the person sitting next to the critic in the theater. There's no reason for critics' reviews to appear day after day as though they have special knowledge.

- A critic should be a representative of the average theatergoer—that's a very widespread attitude among critics.

Marsha Norman: I suppose they probably say that's a way of maintaining their objectivity. I think, that's a way of remaining unaccountable for their ignorance.

HAROLD PRINCE

I was raised to believe that it was immoral to know critics; that *I* do what I do; *they* do what they do, and our paths should never cross. Meeting critics socially raises the possibility that the review is influenced, pro or con, because of it.

- Most of the critics also say that they refrain from being friends with theater people.

Harold Prince: Where do they say that? It's not true. They love invitations to parties. Diverging—here's another problem with contemporary critics: just as the man who reads the news on TV each night has confused himself with the man who makes the news. The critic in America has confused himself with the artist and seeks celebrity. He wants to be a celebrity.

PETER SHAFFER

It would be very difficult for them to avoid compromising their neutrality if they were at rehearsals, or if they started making friends with actors or playwrights. It wouldn't be such a good idea, would it? It would be very hard if you were a critic, and you and I were very good friends, and you gave my play a very bad notice– how would we be able to sustain that relationship afterwards?

- I would be able.

Peter Shaffer: I wouldn't. I wouldn't be interested at all in your objectivity!

AUGUST WILSON

There are critics with whom I'd love to have a conversation, but somehow we can't have it—like they are God. There are a couple whom I can have lunch with. We can talk and that doesn't mean, "O.K., now you got to give me a good review!" In fact, there is one person in particular I'm talking about, with whom I've had lunch, and he gave me a kind of so-so review. But he's free to do that. That has no bearing on me as a person. He's commenting on my art, which is his job.

EMANUEL AZENBERG

If their character was stronger, they wouldn't feel that they were compromised. Of course, they should be a part of the community. Sometimes I have tried to get critics to come out somewhere to see a play to tell me what they think. Nobody comes.

- Some of them say that producers don't allow them.

Emanuel Asenberg: We've invited them and they won't come. I need a good critic. I need somebody who's objective to tell me what's wrong. We are all subjective: the playwright, the director, the actors. Just recently we invited two critics to see Neil Simon's play *Jake's Women* in San Diego. They refused. A man from *The New York Times* came to write a story about Neil Simon, and he wouldn't even give Neil his opinion about the play. Neil yelled at him, "You expect me to say everything to you, and I'm just asking you, "What do your think?" Come on! You know something about the theater. Help!" He said, "It's not the policy of the paper to do that!"

The critics don't really know enough about the process of doing a play. They write, "The direction was wonderful!" How did you know? The man who directed the original company of *Rosencrantz and Guildenstern are Dead* was incompetent and he got rave notices.

ANDRÈ BISHOP

If critics went to rehearsals and were more involved in the process that would be helpful. But I don't see that ever happening in this country, because so much of New York theater is based on economics. Critics don't want to be friends with theater people because they are afraid they'll be accused of being partial.

Part V
Intermission With A Frown:
7 Curious Stories From The Professional
Lives Of Theater–Makers Where Critics
Are Involved

CRITICAL ENCOUNTERS

Emanuel Azenberg

When Neil Simon's *The Odd Couple* was in Boston, it had a very bad 3rd act. The critic Elliot Norton came and he suggested that the Pigeon sisters come back—you can't just have them in the 2nd act—and Neil Simon got on a train from Boston to Baltimore and he wrote a new 3rd act. So the critic was responsible for the 3rd act. There was another critic that we would look for help: Richard Coe in Washington. He would write his review, then he would come over to the table. We'd ask, "What do you think, Dick?" and he'd give us his opinion. David Richards was always very helpful when we would go to Washington before New York. On the other hand, when we went to Washington with *Lost in Yonkers,* there was a critic there who detests Neil Simon, and her opening line was, "Neil Simon has never been able to write a play and he still cannot write a play." Why would we go to Washington now? It's foolish to go there because we are not going to get anything constructive. And then the play turns out to be a big success, and Neil Simon wins the Pulitzer Prize. Perhaps *The Washington Post* should rethink their commitment to this critic.

I don't think the newspapers acknowledge that they make mistakes. They fire people, but it's never a mistake. When we produced *The Lion in Winter,* Stanley Kauffmann was writing for *The New York Times.* He detested the play, and when the movie came out he found it equally loathsome, and the playwright never wrote another play. He said, "This is the best I've got. If they don't like it..." And he wrote films. The famous playwright Paddy Chayevsky also left the theater because of the critics. He said, "Why come and be yelled at like that?"

A THEATER UNDER FIRE

Andrè Bishop

One critic years ago wrote a review about various theaters, including Playwrights Horizons in a monthly magazine. We had a bad season that year and she said in

155

her review that clearly the work of Playwrights Horizons was not good because I was too busy decorating our lobby! It hurt me because I didn't spend *any* time redecorating our lobby—how would she know? And it was not her concern to say so. We happened to have redecorated the lobby that year, but that had nothing to do with me; it just was a year that wasn't very good. Oddly that same critic recently reviewed a musical we'd done and complained about the box-office. She called up and said, "What time does the Sondheim show get out?", and the box-office attendant said, "Oh, you mean *Assassins?*" She took it as if Playwright Horizons had been very pretentious about correcting her. What she didn't know was that we have a very big box-office that handles a lot of different plays in a variety of theaters and they were also selling tickets for another musical by Sondheim. So she criticized us for being "pretentious." That kind of thing drives me crazy. I'm sorry she didn't like the show, but I don't like being told how to do my job by a critic who has no idea of what goes on in the theater. The sadness about most critics is that they may be very smart about plays, but they have no idea about how to run a theater, or what goes on and sometimes they make judgements as if they do.

BETTER LATE THAN NEVER

James Freydberg

Everybody always says to a critic, "You were at that performance, but you should have come to two others." So I had a national critic, now retired, come to see a production of mine on an early preview and he wrote me a review. Then I said, "I want you to come back two more times!" He came and he was shocked how different it was, and he thought that it was one of the most extraordinary lessons that he had ever had.

REVEALING THE SECRET

James Freydberg

Once I had a play that I was very confused about. I don't want to say the playwright's name, because it's a very famous name. We were out of town. I realized that the point of what the play was about was not coming across very well. Seven critics went to see the play. I told two of them beforehand what it was about; what the metaphor was. Five of them I didn't tell. And the two wrote rave reviews; the others wrote terrible reviews. Which proved that I was right. I wanted to get the point across to the author, "Look this is not happening: these two know what it's about because they've been told and these five don't."

A REVIEW FORECAST

Peter Shaffer

When my first play *Five Finger Exercise* opened in New York—after it, there was a party. I was talking to Peter Brook, and the party was going very well. I said, "Maybe such and such—if the play is a success, and if the people like it, and if the notices are good." And he said, "Oh, but the notices *are* good!" I said, "How can you know that?" He said, pointing to all the guests, "Because they are still here! And if the notices hadn't been good, they would have all left." That's how superstitious they are in New York. They don't want to be associated with failure; they'll leave the party. Suddenly it will disappear like snow in August; the guests would all have vanished. Isn't that charming?

CRITICS AND FIRST NIGHT'S MATH AT THE BAR

Peter Shaffer

I remember that on the first night of *The Royal Hunt of the Sun* in New York there was another party, and the first notice was not very good, so they closed the bar. Then the second notice came out, and it looked as if things were going right, so they opened the bar again. Then the third notice came out and it wasn't so good, so they thought of closing the bar again. The man who designed the set—Michael Annals—said, "Four drinks please, because I'm told that there are seven newspapers in this city and three of them already came out. That means four drinks. I don't want to risk not having a drink every time another notice appears." That seems to me to sum up a lot.

Part VI
Thumbs Up!

1   FAVORITE CRITICS: THE CRITICS' CHOICE

Dennis Cunningham
Michael Feingold
William A. Henry III
Holly Hill
Stanley Kauffmann

Edith Oliver
David Richards
Alisa Solomon
Edwin Wilson

They answer the question:

- **Who of your fellow critics do you appreciate most?**

DENNIS CUNNINGHAM

John Simon certainly. I miss Walter Kerr's writing. Nobody has that touch. Every now and then, I'm impressed by Frank Rich. He incidentally is a hell of a good writer. In fact, his review of *Dancing at Lughnasa* captured that play so much that I actually started getting tears in my eyes just reading his review. In TV—nobody. Except, of course, me.

MICHAEL FEINGOLD

One of the most heartening things that's happened in New York recently is the advent of *Newsday,* which really has an excellent theater staff: Linda Winer and Jan Stuart. I don't mean I agree with them all the time, but I always respect their views. They're honest, without hysteria or arrogance; they don't dismiss out of hand things they're experiencing for the first time. I like Jeremy Gerard at *Variety* much the same way. And there are younger critics I like who have intelligent views and a good working knowledge of theater: David Kaufman of *Downtown,* Michael Sommers at the Newark paper, Francine Russo, Marc Robinson, and Brian Parks at *The Village Voice.* I like Alisa Solomon's work very much; occasionally she makes the mistake of letting her aesthetic politics, rather than her taste, preprogram her response. But one would worry about this only if she didn't have a passionate response to art in the first place, so it's a kind of compliment. It's better than the tired old dogs who see theater only as a moneymaking machine; they make me sad. And saddest of all are the youngsters who've been poisoned by the universities into thinking art is a theoretical exercise for the intelligentsia. Jonathan Kalb, who's very bright, is to me a classic example of a good theater mind ruined by academia. I just can't see what he writes as having anything to do with the reality of the art; to me it's dead from the outset and so irrelevant. The pedantry in our colleges has spoiled so many young artists and critics in the last few years that I've come to regard theory—any theory—as essentially totalitarian and inimical to art.

WILLIAM A. HENRY III

Honestly, I don't read anybody that consistently, because I don't want to be overinfluenced. And there are people whom one likes personally but whom one may not be so keen on professionally, or vice versa. Frank Rich, although I disagree with him frequently, is a very good writer. By his own standards and principles, not all of which I agree with, he does an honest job and I consider him deserving. I like the work of Ed Wilson at the *Wall Street Journal*. He's very good. I find I quite frequently agree with Michael Kuchwara of *Associated Press*. Of more scholarly and older critics, Robert Brustein and Richard Gilman have both been teachers and mentors of mine and I think they are true writers. I don't always agree with them, but they have very consistent aesthetics and values, and they clearly engage their own opinions, preferences, and biases in their writing, which is candid and wise. Back among the daily practitioners, Clive Barnes is talented and smart, but he writes too much and so he has good days and bad days.

HOLLY HILL

In New York city the colleagues that I most admire are Linda Winer and Jan Stuart as a combination of critics at *Newsday*. When Sylvianne Gold was writing first for the *New York Post* and then for the *Wall Street Journal,* I thought that she was the best of all writers and not coincidentally she is now the arts editor at *Newsday,* so she would hire critics as knowledgeable as Linda Winer and Jan Stuart. They aren't the flashiest writers, but they are extremely well-informed and well-balanced, and I trust their judgements much more than I trust the judgements of some writers who are flashier. They have in mind the welfare of the readers and the theater community, and themselves as critics; they have a very good balance.

STANLEY KAUFFMANN

Robert Brustein is a critic with worthy seriousness. John Simon must be paid attention to. And one of the best theater critics in this country—Richard Gilman—is not writing theater criticism now. Also, Alisa Solomon, Michael Feingold, Jonathan Kalb, Marc Robinson.

EDITH OLIVER

I enjoy a lot of them. But if I have to be absolutely honest, I never get tired of the theater, but I get awfully tired of opinions about the theater, so I generally skip reviews week after week. My dear friend, Clive Barnes, used to be so offended when I said, "What did you think about this, Clive?" It was inconceivable to him that I hadn't read his review.

DAVID RICHARDS

I like Frank Rich a lot. When I was in Washington, I would read him frequently, even though I wasn't necessarily seeing the shows. I would read him anyway. Just for the experience itself.

ALISA SOLOMON

I have very little appreciation for the daily reviewers. I admire a lot of my colleagues at *The Village Voice*. Gordon Rogoff is a true critic, and I wish Eric Bentley were writing more. Erika Munk is a great writer, but she's not writing now. So they are out there, but there aren't a lot of venues.

EDWIN WILSON

The level of theater is in trouble right now, and the level of criticism, in correlation, is also in trouble. There were several critics whom I admired when I first began: Eric Bentley, Harold Clurman, and to some extent Walter Kerr. I just don't think there are too many people like them writing now.

2   FAVORITE CRITICS:
THE THEATER—MAKERS' CHOICE

Producers:

Andrè Bishop
James Freydberg
Bernard Jacobs
Ellen Stewart
Robert Whitehead

Playwrights:

Marsha Norman
George Wolfe

They answer the question:

- **Who of the critics writing today do you appreciate most?**

ANDRÈ BISHOP

I like Frank Rich. Sometimes I like some of the critics for *The Village Voice:* I don't always agree with it, but there's a stated point of view. I like Edith Oliver because she's very positive, especially about young writers.

JAMES FREYDBERG

Frank Rich is the best critic in New York. Most people feel that he has been destructive to the theater. I don't agree with that. Once you open the show, 80 per cent of it is the marketing of it. Frank Rich's review is only out there for one day. Your job is to present appealing positive views to the audience so that they'll come in. There are a lot of people who feel that what's wrong with him is that he doesn't love the theater and therefore he's highly critical. I don't agree with that either. I think he does love the theater and he's highly critical because he's looking for something above what most people expect. He's not willing to settle for just O.K.

BERNARD JACOBS

Oh, I don't want to get involved in that. I respect Mr. Rich though, by the way. He's an intelligent critic. He's also a very tough critic. He wants to apply standards which he thinks the theater should achieve, but which it may not be possible for it to actually achieve.

ELLEN STEWART

There are several, but I would say: Michael Feingold.

ROBERT WHITEHEAD

Howard Kissel is a good and a thoughtful critic, and a caring one. Frank Rich is quite clever with his language. *The New York Times* feels that he is a stylist. I don't feel he has a style particularly. He has got a way with words, but he's not a good critic, and it's unfortunate in a way, because he's the No. 1. I like Clive Barnes. He tries to help plays to some degree because he knows that the *Times* isn't helping them.

MARSHA NORMAN

Ed Wilson of *The Wall Street Journal* is very good.

I think that you could probably take some of the people that we have writing now and put them through an intense training program to show them what they've been writing about.

GEORGE WOLFE

I really don't like discussing them too much because they have enough power already, and my talking about them—anyone talking about them, gives them even more. I do however appreciate the fact that Frank Rich understands that there is an African American aesthetics at play in my work and August Wilson's work as well as that of other black writers. John Simon, when he isn't being mean, can be quite perceptive. The critics at *The Village Voice,* who pride themselves on being an alternative to the big boys uptown, are just as biased, if not more so.

INDEX